RIGHT OR WRONG?

RIGHT
OR
WRONG?

T. B. Maston

BROADMAN PRESS
Nashville, Tennessee

Copyright, 1955
BROADMAN PRESS
NASHVILLE, TENNESSEE

Thirteenth Printing

422–030

Printed in the United States of America
5.D65KSP

To

*the Christian Youth of Seminary Hill in general
and of Gambrell Street Baptist Church in particular*

Do you ever find it difficult to know whether a particular activity is right or wrong? When you were a child your parents largely decided such matters for you. Now that you are more mature you are discovering that they are shifting the responsibility for such decisions to you. They, along with your teachers and leaders, have sought to build into your life some fundamental principles that will help you to make your decisions wisely.

The discussions in this book represent an attempt to set out some basic principles, principles that you can use to decide for yourself what is right and wrong for you to do. These principles are applied in Part II to some of the more common problems of young people.

It has been assumed throughout these essays or discussions that you are an intelligent Christian youth who wants to know what is right and will be willing to search diligently for the truth or the right. It also has been presupposed that there is such a thing as right and wrong, that one can know the right and wrong, and that the right will always be best for one. The last assumption means that we should search for the right, and, once knowing it, we should joyously seek to do it.

Although written primarily for you and other Christian youth, it is hoped that this material will be helpful to your parents, teachers, and leaders. It may be that some of them will find the discussions usable as a basis for personal counseling and for group conferences.

It is hoped that you will read carefully Part I on basic Christian principles before considering the problems in Part II. It would be better for you to read or study Part I and never read Part II than to read the latter and fail to read the former.

It also is hoped that you will read carefully Part III. It was felt that the conception of the Christian life would be incomplete, if not inaccurate, if some emphasis was not given to the positive phases of that life. This is done in a very brief way in Part III. There also is included an opportunity for you to make a personal application or a committal not only in the areas covered in the different chapters but also in some other important areas of your life and experience as a Christian.

Part IV entitled "A Postscript" includes a closing appeal that we all accept the challenge of Christ to follow him. I trust that you will read this closing chapter which is written for the morally and spiritually mature.

Possibly I should explain to you that there is no attempt in this book to examine every phase of the Christian life. The discussions are restricted, to a large degree, to problems that are considered most consciously and immediatedly acute in your life and in the lives of other Christian youth. It is conceded that there are other important areas of the Christian's life, more positive in the main, that are not touched on at all or at best are only discussed in very general terms. This deliberate limitation will explain the absence in the book of any specific consideration of such matters as your attitude toward and relation to the members of your family or to those of other racial and class groups. It will also explain the fact that there is no specific discussion of the Christian's responsibility to his community, to his nation, and to the world in general. These matters are outside the purpose of the present volume. A discussion of them would require a separate book. This has been done by the author, admittedly in a brief and inadequate way, in a volume written primarily for adults, entitled *The Christian in the Modern World* (Broadman Press, 1952).

May these brief chapters be blessed of the Lord and used by

him to help you to find personally satisfying and Christ-honoring answers to at least some of the perplexing questions and problems of your life. This is my prayer. Will you not help to answer this prayer by approaching the reading and studying of this book with an open mind and with a heart that is willing to follow any light that may come to you from our Heavenly Father?

ACKNOWLEDGMENTS

Many people have contributed in different ways and to varying degrees to the writing of this book. For the title I am indebted indirectly to Dr. E. D. Head, for eleven years the president of Southwestern Baptist Theological Seminary. He preached a sermon some years ago entitled, "Is It Right? Is It Wrong?" Two points of that sermon are the first two tests in the chapter, "Right or Wrong: Three Tests."

A number of friends read the book in manuscript and most of them made suggestions that have led to considerable revision and improvement. Needless to say, none of them is responsible for the contents of the volume or the positions taken in it. All of these friends are busy people and the author is heavily indebted to them for taking the time to read and to appraise the manuscript. Among those who have read the manuscript, all of whom are active in some phase of youth work, are C. F. Barry, J. I. Bishop, Mrs. H. C. Brown, Gainer Bryan, Jr., Margaret Bruce, Versil Crenshaw, Mack Douglas, William Hall Preston, Maines Rawls, Allen R. Watson, and Stanley Williamson.

Two college students, Marilyn McNeely and Clifford Donnelly, friends and neighbors for years, read the manuscript and gave a preview of youth's reaction to the problems discussed. My son, Gene, who is still young enough to have the youth viewpoint, but who also works with young people, has been particularly helpful at many points and in many ways.

A special word of appreciation is expressed to Ola Mae Kemp, who typed the original copies that were sent out for appraisal, and to Mamie Storrs, who has prepared the final copy for the publisher.

Unless otherwise indicated, all Scripture references are from the Revised Standard Version of the Bible, and are used by permission of the copyright owners.

I am particularly indebted to C. Aubrey Hearn for sharing with me some reference books and magazine articles on smoking. Some of this material was used in revising Chapter 13.

CONTENTS

PART III

POSITIVE CHRISTIAN LIVING

PART IV

A POSTSCRIPT

Part I

PRINCIPLES

LEVELS OF LIVING

Have you recently had to make a decision concerning cheating, gambling, Sunday movies, smoking, drinking, dancing, or petting? If so, did you merely drift with the crowd or did you make your decision personally and deliberately? Could you intelligently defend the position you took? If so, what were the arguments you would have given? Have you developed the maturity, the strength, and the stability to stand by your decisions once you have made them? Can you do this without needlessly offending those who disagree with you?

It will be a great blessing to you if you have built into your life some fundamental principles that will give you a basis not only for one but for every decision. These principles if closely enough related or properly unified will make up your philosophy of life. They will not only give you a basis for the decisions of life but they will also give you the poise and strength to face courageously and victoriously life and all that life brings.

This and the other chapters in Part I are written with the hope that they will suggest some principles that you can utilize to make your decisions and to build your philosophy of life. Some of these chapters will not be as easy to read as the ones in Part II. It is assumed, however, that you are intelligent enough and deeply enough interested to read Part I carefully and prayerfully.

The approach in some of these chapters will be more impersonal than in other portions of the book. The principles apply to me and other adults as well as to you and other young people. I trust, however, that you will make the principles personal by applying them to some particular problem you are now facing. As we think together in this chapter concerning the levels of

3

living, will you seek to determine the level on which you think a Christian should live and hence the level on which he should make his decisions?

THE INSTINCTIVE LEVEL

This is the level on which animals live. Many human activities are on the same level. A child's behavior, for example, is largely instinctive. He has certain inborn urges or hungers that determine, to a large degree, what he does. He has the natural urge to eat, to drink, to play, and to seek ways to satisfy these and other desires.

There is nothing wrong with the natural desires or hungers of children. They may be expressed, however, in hurtful ways. While the child is immature and cannot distinguish between wise and unwise ways to express his instincts or hungers, society considers the parents primarily responsible for what he does. For example, parents who carelessly leave a bottle of poison where a child gets it and drinks it, are generally condemned by their neighbors for their carelessness. The child's act is not judged to be a moral act because he did not know any better.

A part of the maturing process is to help the child to understand increasingly the proper limits within which he can express wisely his natural urges or instincts. The adult who does not recognize and adhere to these proper limits is usually considered an undisciplined individual, one who is dangerous to himself and to society. This does not mean that instincts and natural urges do not continue to be important factors in a person's life. Much of the conduct, even of mature Christian men and women, is instinctively based.

There are some people, however, who suggest that every natural urge should be given free expression. They contend that the instinctive thing is the right thing to do. Some even go so far as to argue that if one restrains or curbs any of his natural urges, he will damage his personality. They say that a man "must be free" if he is to develop a creative personality.

Such reasoning reveals a confusion between freedom and li-

cense. One of the surest ways for one to lose his freedom is for
him to give unrestrained expression to every natural urge of his
life. The most severe restriction of freedom comes from the enslavement of sin.

Man, in common with other created beings, finds his greatest
freedom when he fulfils his proper function or functions. Even
the powerful diesel engine that pulls the long string of.freight
cars has its greatest freedom by remaining on the steel rails that
are made for it. Let it jump the track, and it is helpless. Similarly, man finds his greatest freedom when he fulfils most completely the functions or purposes for which God created him. He
discovers real freedom when he lives within the restraining influence of God's laws for him.

We would consider a mother foolish and sinful if she reasoned
as follows: "It is natural for my child to put anything into his
mouth. I must not inhibit him. I must let him express himself
freely." Wise mothers know that the child must be restrained until he can be trained to know what is proper and improper for
him to eat.

In a very real sense, we continue, as we grow older, to be children. We have instincts or native tendencies that are right within
themselves, but they may be expressed in wrong or hurtful ways.
One of the evidences that we are maturing is our progressive
control over these instincts and tendencies, so controlling them
that they find expression only in healthy ways. If expressed in
such ways, they will contribute to the enrichment of our lives,
and to the good of others and of society.

THE CUSTOMARY LEVEL

The word "moral" comes from the Latin word *mores* which
means custom, habit, or tradition. Most of what we do, we do
because it is the generally accepted, the approved, the customary.
It is approved by our family, our church, our community, or our
crowd.

Many young people who pride themselves on their independence are frequently the most abject slaves to their particular

crowd. They may be free from the control of parents and adults. They may ridicule the "mores" or customs of the community, but seldom do they assert real independence of their own age group. In defending certain lines of conduct, no expressions are more frequently used by them than the following: "everybody is doing it," "it is expected," or "you have to gamble to be accepted by the crowd or to be popular." Such statements reveal that they are living on the customary level, although the custom or pattern may be set by a restricted segment of society.

It should not only be admitted but suggested that Christian young people should give serious consideration to what others believe to be right and wrong. They should attach particular importance to the judgment of their parents and to the position of their church. They should weigh carefully the customs and traditions of their community and the viewpoint of their gang or group.

We have not arrived, however, at the highest level of moral living if we simply accept, without thought or reflection, the customary as the final word for our lives. We are individuals who are personally responsible unto God. We should decide for ourselves what is right and wrong for us to do. This is an appeal for what might be called "reflective morality"; for moral conduct that is based on personal thought and judgment. One may conclude that the customary standards are right, but he should not accept them simply because they are customary.

If one lived on the purely customary level, never rising above it, he would not ask the question, "Is it right; is it wrong?" Without raising any question, he would simply accept the customary as the final authority for him. However, even if people wanted to live on the customary level, society is too complicated for such a simple procedure. There are conflicts in the customs.

There are frequently two or more schools of thought concerning a particular issue. For example, various groups of young people will not agree concerning the rightness or wrongness of a particular activity. If one is going to follow the customary, he must choose between customs or traditions. Likewise, one's church may take one position, the community in general and even other churches another, concerning the same problem. Of course, we may make our decision entirely on the basis of our loyalty to a particular group without considering the rightness or wrongness of the custom or tradition. We have not arrived at the highest level of moral living, however, until we have thought through to a defensible position.

THE CONSCIENCE LEVEL

The more intelligent people, young and old, and the ones who contribute the most to lifting the moral level of the world, are those who have thought through to clear-cut personal convictions concerning what is right and wrong for their lives. They follow their own conscience. This does not necessarily mean that they will not accept most of the traditional standards of their homes and their churches. This they may do, but they will do so because they have considered carefully these standards and have come to the conclusion that they are right or true.

Such thinking through of what is right and wrong contributes to stability of character. An individual with personal convictions will not be swept along with every wind that blows. He will not drift with the crowd. There will be times when he will have to go against the crowd, when he will have to buck the current. He will do this, knowing that only those who have the courage and strength of character to swim against the currents of life can ever change the direction of those currents.

This does not mean that Christian young people should pride themselves on being different or peculiar. Neither does it mean that they should become dogmatic, feeling that they, in a unique way or to an unusual degree, know and do the right. There is a fine but important line of distinction between depth of conviction and dogmatism. The former we should have; the latter we should avoid.

If we are wise even in regard to our own convictions, we shall retain a certain element of tentativeness. We should maintain an open mind. New insights may come to us. What we consider right today, we may consider wrong tomorrow. This will not be necessarily a sign of instability. It may be an evidence of growth.

We have not said much concerning the meaning of conscience. That is a technical matter that does not concern us in this book. We are using the term rather loosely. Man by nature has a sense of oughtness in life. He innately feels that there is such a thing as right and wrong.

While the inner conviction that there is such a thing as right and wrong is innate or inborn, the content of the rightness and wrongness is not innate. The content of what we term conscience is determined for each man by his total moral experience: by the decisions he has made in the past, by his family background, his community relations, and other influences that have touched his life.

Young people frequently ask, "Can I trust my conscience? Will it always lead me aright?" What are the answers to these questions? We must admit that one may be entirely conscientious concerning a matter and yet be wrong. Paul evidently persecuted the Christians in good conscience. Many men have done things just as bad and considered them right.

If conscience is not to be trusted, should we do what it tells us to do? Possibly we should make a distinction between the inerrancy and the authority of one's conscience. Conscience is not inerrant or infallible. It may and will make mistakes, but we can accept its authority provided we are constantly striving to educate it toward right attitudes and higher levels. Only those who follow the best they can what they consider right will have additional insight into new areas of truth.

THE CHRISTIAN LEVEL

The Christian level of living is the highest level. Only when man lives on the Christian level does he become most completely man, realizing in himself the divinely ordained potential for his life. There is no necessary conflict, however, between the Christian level of living and the other levels that have been discussed.

The main difference is that the one who lives on the Christian level makes Christian principles or ideals the final test for every decision concerning what is right and wrong for his life. For example, he may accept the customs of the family, the church, and the community, but he will do so because he finds that they conform to Christian standards. One who seeks to be a real Christian and to apply the spirit and teachings of Jesus to his life may follow his conscience, but his conscience will be a Christian conscience. It will have a point of reference different from the conscience of a non-Christian. The true Christian accepts God's basic moral and spiritual principles as authoritative for his conscience.

Another important characteristic of the Christian level of living is the fact that the Christian not only has his conscience to guide him, but he has the Holy Spirit to inform and to guide his conscience. In other words, the Spirit is given to the Christian to guide him into all the truth (John 16:13). Any time he lacks wisdom he can "ask God who gives to all men generously and without reproaching, and it will be given him" (James 1:5).

The Bible and the Holy Spirit are two forces or factors in the Christian's life that the non-Christian does not have. It is true that the non-Christian can read his Bible and may receive considerable help from it, but he does not and cannot have the leadership of the Spirit in interpreting the Bible and in applying its truth to the problems and needs of his life. These two, the Bible and the Holy Spirit, should be major factors in determining for the Christian what he considers to be right and wrong. If followed sincerely, they will give to his life a tone and quality different from the non-Christian's. His life will not be conformed to the world but will be transformed or transfigured (Rom. 12:2) and will become a transforming influence in the world. He will live in the world and yet be separated spiritually from the world.

2

THE CHRISTIAN AND HIS STEWARDSHIP

If we accept the basic principles of Christian stewardship, they will help us to decide whether or not a particular activity is right or wrong. The following are some elements in an adequate conception of Christian stewardship.

THE STEWARD

The proper place to begin a study of stewardship is with the steward himself. We, who are Christians, are not our own; we have been bought with a price (1 Cor. 6:19–20), and that price was the death of Christ on the cross. Paul spoke of himself as the bondservant or slave of Christ (Rom. 1:1; Phil. 1:1; Titus 1:1, and elsewhere). He also suggested that the only way for one to win his freedom from Satan and from the bondage of sin was for him to become the slave of Christ and of righteousness (Rom. 6:15–23).

How glorious it is, however, that we who are slaves of Christ have been made stewards in his household. He has entrusted his work to us. We can become colaborers or fellow workers with God in his work in the world (1 Cor. 3:9). What a privilege and responsibility it is!

As we contemplate our stewardship, let us never forget that we belong to God. He has the right to command. In his goodness he has invited us to co-operate with him.

THE STEWARD AND MATERIAL POSSESSIONS

Although this phase of stewardship is not as closely related to the problems we are dealing with in these discussions as are some other phases, yet the picture would not be complete without at least a brief consideration of the stewardship of things material.

Since we belong to God, it follows inevitably that all we have belongs to him. This means that if we are thoroughly convinced that we are stewards, it will not be hard to persuade us of our stewardship of our material possessions.

Then, if all we have belongs to God, it naturally follows that we should give liberally to support the cause of Christ. We should not give less than a tithe. It is also important and normal that we should acknowledge that the remainder of our income and all of our material goods belong to God and are to be used in God-honoring ways. Also included in any adequate conception of Christian stewardship is the way we make our money.

THE STEWARD AND HIS BODY

If we belong to Christ, then our bodies belong to him and are a part of our stewardship privilege and responsibility. Paul states it plainly for us when he says, "The body is . . . for the Lord, and the Lord for the body. . . . Do you not know that your bodies are members of Christ? . . . Do you not know that your body is a temple [tabernacle or dwelling place] of the Holy Spirit" (1 Cor. 6:13, 15, 19).

In the letter to the Roman church, Paul, on the basis of what he had said in the preceding eleven chapters, exhorted the Roman Christians as follows: "I appeal to you therefore, brethren, by the mercies of God, to present your bodies as a living sacrifice, holy and acceptable to God, which is your spiritual worship" (Rom. 12:1). The body can and should be holy; it can and should be acceptable unto God; it can and should be used to serve God and to bless our fellow man.

A clear understanding of the stewardship of our bodies will help us to reach wise decisions concerning the rightness or wrongness of many of the activities we face every day. We may consider the physical level a rather low basis on which to make a decision, but, whether it is low or not, many of our problems could be settled for us on that level.

One of the glorious things about Christian stewardship is the fact that things material and physical can be used for spiritual purposes. For example, the body is an absolutely essential channel or instrument if the work of the Lord is to be done in the world. This dignifies and glorifies the body of the Christian.

THE STEWARD AND HIS PERSONALITY

The body is a phase, but only a phase, of one's personality. In one sense it would be more correct to consider the body as an instrument or channel through which one's personality finds expression in relation to his fellows. At least personality cannot be identified with physical appearance.

By "personality" we mean to include such things as one's native mental capacity, disposition, temperament, talents, attitudes, and other things that make him a distinct individual or person. Some of these things are a part of us because of our heritage or our environment. For example, one person may be born with limited mental ability while another may be decidedly superior. They are not accountable for their much or little ability. They are responsible to God and to society for what they do with what they have. So it is with other phases of our personalities. This is a part of our total stewardship.

THE STEWARD AND HIS TIME

This is another important phase of the stewardship life. If we belong to God—and we do if we are children of his—then we are responsible unto him for what we do with the time he gives us. This does not mean that all of it is to be used in specific Christian service. Some time is required for eating and sleeping. We also know that our bodies need a certain amount of sunshine and play or recreation if they are to be in the best condition for service. Also, some recreation and social fellowship are necessary if we are to have well-balanced personalities and are to maintain healthy attitudes toward life.

A wise stewardship of time will mean that we shall avoid using any of our time for activities destructive of our own best selves, hurtful to others, or that reflect discredit on the cause of Christ.

As we mature as Christians, we shall have a deepening conviction that an increasing proportion of our time should be used for service to our fellow man and God. Sooner or later we shall awaken to the fact that what we are going to do for God and mankind must be done in a hurry. This gives to us a sense of holy urgency.

We shall guard against a waste of time. We shall continue to recognize the need for the proper amount of time for rest, relaxation, and social fellowship, but we shall consider all of these as preparatory to more effective service. They will no longer be ends, of value within themselves, but means, of value because they contribute to a more effective service to God and man.

THE STEWARD AND HIS INFLUENCE

Here we are getting to a phase of stewardship that is somewhat more intangible but of tremendous significance. We are responsible unto God for our influence. Our influence is counting for good or bad, to a lesser or a greater degree, on all we touch.

This phase of stewardship, as is true of other phases, involves both a great privilege and a great responsibility. We may not be able to preach like our pastor, sing on a par with our favorite soloist, or teach as well as the best teacher in our Sunday school, but we can live a consistent Christian life. This is one of God's best gifts, and it is available to all his children, whether they have one or ten talents. We should remember that more people are influenced for Christ by the lives of Christians than by all the sermons preached, the songs sung, or the lessons taught. We can, if we will, have a part in God's most effective way to reach people for himself.

Every child of God, regardless of how young or old, is influencing others. There is always the probability that each one of us is influencing someone else, Christian or non-Christian, more than anyone else who touches that life. How tragic if our influence leads them away from God. How glorious if our influence is used by the Lord to lead them to himself or into a closer walk with him.

THE STEWARD AND THE GOSPEL

Another important aspect of stewardship is the stewardship of the gospel. All other phases of stewardship find their completion and fulfilment in the trusteeship of things spiritual.

What is meant by the stewardship of the gospel? The gospel is good news. It is the good news that Jesus Christ came into the world "to seek and to save the lost" (Luke 19:10); "that whoever believes in him should not perish but have eternal life" (John 3:16); that "he is able for all time to save those who draw near to God through him" (Heb. 7:25); and that "him who comes to me I will not cast out" (John 6:37).

This good news is committed to the children of God, to the disciples of Christ. His command is that we go, and that as we go we shall be his witnesses (Matt. 28:18–20; Acts 1:8).

We can go with the assurance that "every one who calls upon the name of the Lord will be saved." But we should remember the words that follow: "But how are men to call upon him in whom they have not believed? And how are they to believe in him of whom they have never heard? And how are they to hear without a preacher? And how can men preach unless they are sent?" (Rom. 10:13–15).

This means that some Christian stewards should go, some should help them to go, but each one has his particular responsibility for sharing the gospel with the whole world.

In addition to the preceding, each Christian steward has a direct, immediate responsibility to share the good news with those he touches from day to day. He should do this by word of mouth; but what is of equal if not greater importance, he should make known to others the good news in Christ by the life he lives before them in the classroom, on the bus, on the athletic field, in the home, as well as in the church. Our time, our talents, our influence, our bodies, our total personalities, our material means are all to be dedicated to making Christ a living reality in our own lives, in the lives of others, and in every area of our society.

It was Peter who admonished those to whom he was writing

to be "good stewards of God's varied grace" (1 Peter 4:10). It was Paul who spoke of the "stewards of the mysteries [things hidden to the uninitiated but clear to Christians] of God" and then added, "moreover it is required of stewards that they be found trustworthy" (1 Cor. 4:1–2).

This is a big program for Christian youth. But young people are accustomed to and challenged by big programs. Christian youth must respond to the high demands of the gospel if the Christian movement is to make the impact it should on our world. If that impact is not made, it is possible that our nation, Western civilization, and even our world will collapse. In other words, our response to the challenge of Christian stewardship may be worldwide in its significance. Are we being and will we be good, trustworthy stewards?

When we face decisions concerning the rightness or wrongness of some activity, let us remember that we are stewards of God, responsible unto him for what we do with our money, our time, our influence, our total personality, including our body. Most of all, let us never forget that we are stewards of the gospel, of the good news that has brought salvation to us and will bring salvation to all others who will hear and appropriate its message to themselves.

3

SOURCES OF WRONG

Serious-minded, sincerely searching young Christians frequently ask, "What is wrong with cheating, drinking, or dancing? Why do so many people consider it wrong?" Such questions are natural and normal. They are not necessarily a sign of moral immaturity or perverseness. Similar questions are asked frequently by mature Christian men and women. Decisions concerning right and wrong are not limited to any age group.

We should admit, in the beginning, that there are activities that are not wrong within themselves, but participation in them is considered questionable by many Christians. Why should one's participation in such activities be labeled questionable or wrong when the activity within itself is not necessarily wrong or bad? What are some of the things that make participation in particular activities unwise or wrong for the Christian? Such questions are legitimate and should be answered.

ASSOCIATION

There are some things that may seem to be harmless; but they become questionable, if not positively wrong, for Christians because of the environment in which they usually are found or because of their association with other activities that generally are considered wrong. For example, some people argue that there is nothing wrong with a deck of playing cards. Let us assume that their conclusion is correct. There are, on the other hand, many Christians who strongly contend that a Christian should not participate in games that require the use of playing cards. What has caused the deck of cards to have such a bad reputation? One reason frequently given is that cards have been used through the centuries for gambling purposes. Many people, when they see playing cards, immediately associate them with gambling. This association has become so general that many Christians believe that one cannot play cards without hurting his influence for good although he may consider the game an innocent pastime.

Another activity that some consider a good game, but which has become questionable if not actually wrong for a Christian, is the game of pool or billiards. Many who play it say that it is a splendid game, requiring considerable skill to play it successfully. On the other hand, most consecrated Christians consider it unwise or wrong to participate in the game. Why is this true? They suggest that this is true because of the bad environment in which the game is usually played. Frequently, the pool halls are the most unwholesome places in the community. Their reputation became so bad in at least one Southern state that the state legislature outlawed them. When any activity has such a bad name, it is doubtful if Christians can afford to participate in it. The Christian's personal reputation is involved, but what is more important, the good name of his church and of the cause of Christ is at stake. This may even raise a question concerning the wisdom or the rightness of a Christian family providing a pool table in the home.

Activities that usually are found in a bad environment are wrong or unwise for the Christian, not only because participation in them would hurt his influence, but also because of the temptations that so frequently press upon him as a result of his participation. Can you think of activities, other than those mentioned, that are not wrong within themselves but have become questionable for Christians because of their association with other activities or because of the environment in which they are usually found?

ATTITUDE OF OTHERS

This is another reason why some activities that may be considered entirely innocent or harmless by some people may become unwise or wrong for a Christian to indulge in. The Christian is not supposed to please himself but to do those things that can be blessed by the Lord and that will bring a blessing to others. It may sound strange, but the Christian should not let others tell him what is right; that is a personal decision. Yet he should be so sensitive to the moral and spiritual well-being of others that he will let them decide, to a considerable degree, what is wrong for him to do. Even if he thinks a particular activity is entirely all right, he will not participate in it if it will be an offense or a cause of stumbling to others. This will be true because, having caught something of the spirit of his Master, he thinks primarily of others rather than of himself.

This does not mean that we can or should attempt to satisfy every crank. It does mean that for us, as Christians, the attitude of people generally may and should be an important factor in determining what is right or wrong for us to do.

WRONG WITHIN ITSELF

Some people contend that the whole matter of right and wrong is relative, that there are no activities that are wrong within themselves. Such a conclusion is far from the truth.

There are great areas of life that are governed or controlled by moral absolutes. The basic moral laws of God are not dependent upon the environment, the association, or the attitude of people. His fundamental laws are written into our natures and into the nature of the universe in which we live. We are held accountable for the observance of them, although they may not have been incorporated into the statutes of the land.

The Ten Commandments represent a summary of much of the moral law. Some of the Commandments have become a part of the legal code of practically all of the nations of the world. However, this fact is not what makes them right or wrong.

It is wrong to kill, to steal, to commit adultery, to bear false witness, and to covet regardless of what the law of the land may say. There are some things that are wrong within themselves. Man cannot do those things without violating something that is fundamental in himself and in his world. His participation in them is self-defeating to him and destructive of the best there is in society.

There are considerable areas of life that are governed by basic laws that are not included in the Ten Commandments. For example, there are certain health laws. Those laws must be observed, if one is to discover the sources of abiding health. Like the other underlying laws of life, they carry their own penalty. One cannot violate them without paying the price sooner or later. These health laws are among the absolutes of life. To do anything that would break one of them, and thus undermine one's health, is wrong within itself. Its rightness or wrongness does not depend upon what others may think or how they may react.

Will you agree that there are some activities participated in by young people that are wrong within themselves, that violate the fundamental laws of life? What are some such activities?

Right: Absolute and Relative

We have suggested, in answer to the question "What makes an activity wrong?" that some activities are wrong within themselves, but that other activities that may not be wrong as such become wrong for the Christian because of the attitude of others, because of the environment in which those activities are usually found, or because of the purposes for which they are ordinarily used. In other words, some things are wrong within themselves, while others are made wrong by something that is not inherent in the activity but is exterior to it.

This suggests that right and wrong may be relative. If what is wrong is determined by the attitude of others, one might conclude that it may be right to participate in a particular activity in one community but wrong in another. Such a conclusion would be correct. But we need to notice one thing: While that which is right in itself may become wrong because of the attitude of others and the general environment in which the activity is ordinarily found, an activity that is wrong within itself can never be made right because of the environment in which it may be found or the attitude of people toward it. That which is right may become wrong, but that which is wrong can never become right.

This means among other things that a Christian would never be justified in doing a thing he considered wrong, simply because the crowd he was with or people in general considered it right. Such would be a violation of his conscience or his Christian convictions. That route would lead to moral decay and decline rather than to moral growth and advancement.

Even when the right or wrong is relative rather than absolute, there is underneath an absolute principle. For example, one basis for the position that what is right may become wrong is the fact that the Christian should not give primary consideration to what he thinks to be right, but to what effect his participation in an activity will have on others and on the cause of Christ. The preceding sentence states an absolute, a constant, or an unchanging principle. This principle will help one to decide what is right or wrong for him to do concerning activities that he may consider harmless within themselves.

To illustrate the relation of the absolute and the relative, let us consider the game of dominoes. Let us assume—which some Christians will not—that there is nothing wrong with playing dominoes. But you find yourself in a community where the game has a bad reputation. In that community it is generally felt that Christians should not play dominoes and, if they do, that it will hurt their influence. Thus, an activity that may be considered innocent and even wholesome becomes positively wrong for a Christian. Whether playing dominoes is right or wrong is thus relative, since in one situation it might be all right, and in another community it would be wrong. The absolute or the abiding element in such a decision would be the fact that whether or not you played dominoes would be decided on the basis of what influence your participation would have on others and on the cause of Christ, rather than on the basis of your own personal desires.

Thus we can conclude that right and wrong are not absolute *or* relative, but may be both relative *and* absolute. There are some things or activities that are always right or wrong. This is true regardless of the attitude of people toward them. These absolutes are written into the nature of men as moral beings and into the nature of the moral universe in which men live. In contrast, there are broad areas of life covered largely by the relative; right and wrong are not inherent in the act or activity itself, but they are dependent on the effects one's participation may have. We have suggested previously that underneath the relative will be discovered an absolute principle which gives consistency and stability even to the areas largely governed by the relative.

4

DETERMINANTS OF RIGHT

Just as there is more than one factor that may make an activity wrong, so there is more than one theory concerning the determinant of the right or the source of final authority for man. If we determine what will be the utimate source or sources of right in our lives, we will have a dependable basis for decisions concerning the right and wrong in specific areas of our lives.

In the main, there are two questions, each with a supplementary or corollary question, asked by students of human behavior. The questions are: "What is good?" with the corollary question "How can man attain the good?"; or "What is right?" with a corollary question "How can man know and do the right?" The latter pair of questions represents the usual Christian approach to the study of morality or ethics.

THE INDIVIDUAL

Regardless of which of the two preceding approaches—the good or the right—is made, one answer frequently given to the question of final authority is that the individual determines for himself what is good or right. He contains within himself, so it is claimed, the resources to determine and to attain the good; to know the right, and—at least to a reasonable degree—to do the right.

Some would suggest that the individual's own personal pleasure or happiness is the test of whether or not a particular thing is good or right. This position, called hedonism, was common among the Greeks and is still quite prevalent. Some would emphasize the greatest happiness of the greatest number, which is called social hedonism or utilitarianism.

There are others who say that the good or the right thing for man to do will contribute the maximum to his own self-realization. That which enables man to function most completely as man, to develop his innate capacities, is considered right for him.

Still others claim that the right is what man's reason dictates. If man thinks through the problem he faces and decides that a certain thing is right for him to do, it is right.

There are some scholars who believe that man was born with special equipment for moral conduct. They may think of it as a special God-given faculty and may call it "conscience," or, in a rather general sense, they may say that man naturally or innately knows what is right and wrong. Regardless of the term they use or the content they put into it, they contend that the final determiner of right and wrong for a man is within man. This makes moral conduct a strictly individual matter.

Can man be so trusted? Do we not need to remember that he is contaminated with sin and that sin affects every area of his life: his mind and his conscience (at least its content), along with all other phases of his total personality? He cannot be trusted to think straight at all times. Even his conscience (whatever that means) may lead him astray. It is not an infallible guide.

THE GROUP

There are other people who contend that the group should determine what is right and wrong for all individuals in the group. For them, the group should be the final source of authority. This view is very prevalent among primitive peoples. The clan or the tribe, sometimes with great pressure, maintains the mores or traditions of the group. Every member of the clan or tribe must conform.

In more complex societies the pressure to conform is not so strong. There are frequently competing groups whose standards and ideals are not the same. However, there continues considerable emphasis, in one way or another, on a group-type of morality. The group emphasis is most prevalent in the smaller face-to-face groups such as the family, the gang, the play group, or the comparatively isolated rural neighborhood group. Something of this emphasis is seen in the church. The smaller the church, the greater is the pressure ordinarily to conform to group standards.

There are some religious groups that go so far as to claim the right to determine for their adherents what is right and wrong. This is the general position of the Roman Catholic Church. The individual member is limited in his right to decide for himself what is right and wrong. When the group—in this case, the Church—has spoken, its word is final.

Those who contend for the authority of the group in the field of morality usually claim that "the voice of the people is the voice of God." "The people" may be the community as a whole or some particular segment of the community such as the family, the gang, or the church.

We do not accept the voice of the people as authoritative in other areas; why should we in the realm of moral conduct? The people in general do not decide what is good art or music.

Also, experience has taught us that the group cannot be trusted to be right at all times. Really, in the area of moral conduct the crowd will more frequently be wrong than right. Unfortunately the church itself may be wrong on moral issues.

THE WILL OF GOD

If neither the individual nor the group is the proper source of final authority for the right, what is? Our answer is that the only competent determinant for right and wrong for man is the will of God. Our conclusion is that the right is not necessarily what man's reason dictates but what God commands. It is not what man intuits but what the divine voice says. It is not what society sanctions but what the sovereign God approves.

This means that the most important and fundamental question that any Christian can ask when faced with a decision concerning what is right or wrong is: "What is the will of God?" This does not mean that there will be a necessary conflict between the will of God and what one's own common sense would suggest or what his home, his church, or even his group or gang would approve. It does mean that a Christian should make his decision primarily on the basis of what he considers to be the will of God. The other approaches to the right will be supplemental and will be evaluated in the light of what one interprets to be the will of God.

THE NATURE OF THE WILL OF GOD

Before we ask "How can I know the will of God?" let us make two or three general statements concerning the nature of the will of God.

God's will is all-inclusive. It includes what we do (our vocation or profession), where we do it (at home or abroad), the one with whom we walk life's pathway (our companion), and what we are (the life we live every day in every relation of our lives). This indicates that the will of God is much broader, deeper, and more meaningful than we usually think.

God's will is a continuing experience. Frequently, one decision is preparatory to another. If we are responsive to the leadership of the Lord, we shall have a deepening understanding of his will. This, when properly understood, will tend to give us a constant sense of tentativeness, of expectancy, of open-mindedness.

Today we may consider a particular activity in accord with the will of God for our lives. If we are obedient to him, we may discover tomorrow that he has led us to new insights, and that which we once considered right we will then understand to be wrong.

God's will is always best. His will is not only always best for him and his cause; it is always best for us also. If we are serious about doing his will, we may discover that we shall have to give up some things that we now do. There is one thing, however, about which we can be sure. What he requires us to give up is not best for us. This means that his will is not arbitrary. It is in accord with our natures and in harmony with the nature of the society God wills for the world.

Since God's will is always best, we should seek to know his will;

and, once knowing it, we should joyously co-operate with it. If we do this, it will seem at times that we pay dearly for our obedience. That may be true, but it will cost far more, in the long run, to fail to co-operate with the will of God. God has his martyrs, but Satan has many more. God's martyrs are joyous, singing martyrs, while Satan's martyrs are sad and sorrowful.

A missionary expressed this idea as follows: "God has so ordered things that we cannot make a real sacrifice for him." It may and does cost something to follow Jesus, but it also "pays to serve Jesus, it pays every day, it pays every step of the way." Jesus expressed the same idea by stating what, in many ways, is the basic principle or law of life: "For whoever would save his life will lose it, and whoever loses his life for my sake will find it" (Matt. 16:25).

How to Know the Will of God

How can we know the will of God when we are faced with a decision concerning what is right or wrong? It is not always easy. But if we sincerely want to know and are willing to do the will of God, we can and will have enough light to make the immediate decision. When other decisions have to be made, additional light will be given.

All of us know that the chief tangible source for a knowledge of the will of God is the Bible. We find in the Bible a record of God's revelation or disclosure of himself to man; a self-disclosure that was climaxed in his Son who was "the very stamp of his nature" (Heb. 1:3). It was Jesus himself who said: "He who has seen me has seen the Father" (John 14:9), and, "I and the Father are one" (John 10:30).

We find revealed in the Bible not only the nature and character of God but also his attitude toward and his will for man. By the latter, we do not mean that we can turn to a particular chapter and verse for an answer in every time of decision. The Bible is not a rule book. Yet, if we study it consistently, prayerfully, and obediently, we shall receive much direct and much more indirect help from it. The Bible is such an important factor in our knowledge of God and his will that it is safe to say that a Christian cannot know God's will as he should, in a time of decision, unless he has prepared himself for such a time by saturating himself in the Word of God, unless he has sought through a study of that Word to know the mind of Christ.

What can the Christian do when he cannot find a specific word in the Bible in a time of decision? He has the promise of the leadership of the Holy Spirit. One of the Spirit's functions is to teach us or to reveal to us the truth.

One way a study of the Bible helps us is to make our spiritual ears more sensitive. As we become more spiritually minded we are more able to hear "the still small voice" of the Spirit of God as he seeks to speak to us and to lead us.

It is essential if we are to know the will of God that we be willing to do it. It was Jesus who said "if any man's will is to do his will, he shall know whether the teaching is from God or whether I am speaking on my own authority" (John 7:17). After we have sincerely sought to know the will of God, there may remain an element of uncertainty. We can be assured in such times, if we are willing to do his will and start to move in the direction that we have interpreted to be the will of God, that the Lord will not permit us to go far astray. Even in the process of interpreting his will, we should keep our minds and hearts open for additional light, our faces set toward the open road of God's fuller revelation.

Some of you discerning young people may be saying: "The preceding sounds like the source of right after all is in the individual. You have come back to an individual emphasis." The latter is true, but the former does not necessarily follow.

The will of God is the final source of authority for man. The problem we have been dealing with in the immediately preceding paragraphs is the content of that will. We have suggested, or at least implied, that the individual has the right and the responsibility to decide for himself what the will of God is for him. He cannot shift this responsibility to someone else or to any group to which he belongs—family, gang, or church. If he is wise, he will give serious consideration to what these and others have to say, but the final decision is his.

There is no Christian concept more basic to Protestantism in general than this idea of the responsibility of the individual. The individual Christian is to decide for himself what is right and wrong. He has direct access to God without the necessity of going through a priest or the church. This is involved in the idea of the "priesthood of the believer."

Applied to the problems we shall consider later, this means that you, as you mature, will have to decide for yourself what you should do about cheating, petting, smoking, drinking, dancing, and other problems of life. These things you are to decide in the light of what you consider to be the will of God for your life.

Let us never forget, however, that the right to decide for ourselves what is the will of God for our lives involves a tremendous responsibility. We shall be held accountable by our Heavenly Father and by life, as God has ordered it, for the decisions we make. This should give to each one of us a deep sense of the need for divine guidance. We should pray that our decisions will be in accord with God's holy will since we know that it will always be best for us, for those we love, for our friends, our church, our world, and for the cause of Christ.

It is wise, particularly while we are young and immature, to seek the counsel and help of parents and other adult Christians when we are making a decision concerning the will of God in any area of our lives. We should remember, however, that the ultimate responsibility for the decision is ours, that if a mistake is made we have to pay the price.

5

RIGHT OR WRONG:
Three Questions

This and the two succeeding chapters will be more help-ful if you will consider them as a unit. They belong together. They merely represent different ways of approaching the same problem, of attempting to answer the same question. There is, however, a sense in which the chapters supplement each other. Each chapter, with its rather distinctive approach, may be more helpful than either of the others to particular individuals. But it is hoped that you will be helped, to some degree, by them all.

The benefit you will receive from the study of these chapters, and of this entire book, will be determined largely by whether or not you sincerely want to be helped. None of us can be helped in any area of our lives, in any time of decision, unless we search honestly and fearlessly for the right with a deep determination to do what we are persuaded is right regardless of what it may be. Even God will not and cannot reveal his will to a closed mind or an unwilling heart.

Now, let us give attention to three questions that have helped many people in times of decision. These questions are not only applicable to the problems we shall discuss in Part II but to other problems or decisions we may face. They will be helpful not only to young Christians but to older ones as well. The latter may not have the same problems as younger people, but they have their own distinctive problems, many of which are of serious proportions.

THE EFFECT ON US

When we are considering whether or not we should do a cer-tain thing, let us start on the lowest level by asking the question

"How will my participation in this activity affect me as an individual?" This wisely can and should be followed with a series of other questions that will help us to answer more accurately the original question.

Some of the additional questions are: "How will my participation affect my body? Will it contribute to good health and to the building of a strong body, or will it tend to undermine my health and weaken my body?" The physical may seem to be a very low level on which a Christian should begin his search for what is right. In one sense it is, but there is another sense in which it is not.

The body is far more important than many of us realize. The body we have will be an asset or a liability to us all of our lives regardless of what we may do for a vocation. A healthy body is a wonderful servant or instrument; a sickly, weak body can be a terrible master. We should not participate in anything that will endanger our health or prevent the normal development and maturing of our physical selves.

We should also ask ourselves how our participation in this activity might affect our minds, our social natures, our total personalities. Would our participation enrich or impoverish our lives? The mental, social, and spiritual phases of our personalities are even more important, in some ways, than our bodies. We have given more space to the latter primarily because that is the beginning point for our search for the right and because the physical is so frequently neglected or misinterpreted.

As Christians, we must even go beyond the consideration of the effects of our participation upon our bodies, our minds, and our moral nature. These are important but there is another phase of our total personalities that is more important. We are not merely physical bodies with minds and social natures. We are spiritual beings made in the image of God, who find our highest fulfilment in fellowship with him. Our bodies, minds, and social natures should be instruments to be used by the spiritual self to promote spiritual ends. We need to ask: "How will my participation in this activity affect my spiritual life? Will it deepen or lessen my interest in things spiritual? Will it increase or decrease my sense of fellowship with my Heavenly Father?"

We likewise should consider the effects of our participation on our relation to our church and on our prayer and devotional life. These things we will consider if we are serious about being real Christians instead of being just another ordinary, mediocre, or nominal Christian, and if we want to play on God's first team, not being satisfied to play on the "B" squad.

The Effect on Others

We admittedly started at the lowest level for the Christian. A higher level is represented by the question: "How will my participation in this activity affect others and my influence on others?" Other supplementary questions that might be asked are: "Is it possible that my participation may be a cause of stumbling to a weaker Christian?" "May it needlessly be a factor in tempting someone who is not as mature as I am?" "Will my participation make it easier or more difficult for me to witness to unsaved friends about Christ?" "Will the unsaved expect me to do this thing?" Will you agree that these and similar questions should be asked by a Christian in a time of decision?

Many times young Christians and older ones say, "I cannot see any harm in drinking or dancing. I do not think it hurts me to do it." But is that the level on which a Christian should make his final decision concerning what is right for him to do? Far more important than the question "Does it or will it hurt me?" is the question "Does it or will it hurt others and my influence for good on others?"

Paul's principle of eating meat or food offered to idols will provide some helpful guidance at this point (Rom. 14:13–23; 1 Cor. 8:1–13). There are three main things that Paul says: (1) There was nothing wrong with eating the meat, as such. (2) However, if one ate the meat and thus sinned against the conscience of a weaker brother, he sinned against Christ. (3) Paul personally concluded that if by eating the meat he would cause a weaker brother to stumble, he would never eat meat again.

The preceding represents rather strong medicine, but Christians should be willing to take strong medicine. If Paul's principle is followed sincerely, we may and doubtless shall discover that we shall have to give up some activities that we have considered perfectly all right.

We also may find that we could participate in an activity in one community and not in another because of existing difference in attitude toward our participation. Let us repeat, however, what was said in a previous chapter: The attitude of people toward what we do will not and cannot make right that which is wrong within itself. The right may become wrong, but the wrong can never become right.

It is rather important to make the preceding distinction. The attitude of people does not determine what is ultimately right; their attitude may determine whether or not a particular activity is wise or right for us in a given situation. We, as Christians, should give serious consideration to the judgment of people around us primarily because we are interested in the moral and spiritual welfare of those we touch. Paul expressed it as follows: "Do not, for the sake of food, destroy the work of God. Everything is indeed clean, but it is wrong for any one to make others fall by what he eats" (Rom. 14:20). We can substitute for the word "food" any activity concerning which we are attempting to make a decision. Man, who is God's work, or creation, is far more important than one's participation in this or that activity.

THE EFFECT ON THE CAUSE OF CHRIST

The highest level for a decision by a Christian is reached when he asks, "How will my participation in this activity affect the cause of Christ?" This certainly is a very high standard. Will you not concede, however, that every Christian should be willing to ask this question and seek as best he can to answer it honestly?

Some similar questions that we might ask ourselves are: "Can the Lord bless and use for his glory my participation in this activity?" Paul said to the Corinthian Christians: "So, whether you eat or drink, or whatever you do, do all to the glory of God. Give

no offense to Jews or to Greeks or to the church of God" (1 Cor.
10:31-32).

If Paul were writing to your church or mine today, do you
suppose he would put in some other words in the place of "eat"
and "drink"? Do you suppose he would include the word "play"?
Doubtless so, because so many of our problems are in the area of
amusements and recreation. Paul related his teachings to the immediate needs and problems of people. We believe he would do
the same today if he were writing to contemporary churches.

Should we not ask ourselves: "Will this activity be an occasion
of stumbling or will it give offense to the church of God?" Paul
suggests that the child of God, in determining what is right for
him to do, should go beyond himself and even beyond other individuals and should consider the effect of his actions upon the
church which is the body of Christ. Good questions for us to ask
would be: "Will my participation in the activity I am considering make it more or less difficult for my church to do its work
in my community and in the world? Will it reflect credit or discredit upon my church and the cause of Christ in general?"

When Christ has done so much for us, should we not be willing
and even anxious to avoid anything that would be an embarrassment to him or would hurt his cause among men? When the
Christian cause is being challenged by a movement such as communism, whose young people are willing to die for it, Christ's
young people, if they are to meet that challenge, must match the
Communist devotion with an equal willingness to live unselfishly and, if necessary, to die for Christ and his kingdom. This is
a call to high duty, but the days in which we live demand un-
stinted devotion and selfless living. I am persuaded that many,
and I hope most, Christian youth are ready to respond to that
challenge.

Conclusion

The three questions that have been suggested, along with the
supplementary questions, represent progressively higher levels.
The glorious thing is that God has so ordered things that, when

properly interpreted, there can be no real conflict in the conclusions we reach on these different levels. In other words, if we make our decisions on the highest level—the effect on the cause of Christ—we shall discover that they are best not only for the cause of Christ but also for others and even for ourselves. The psalmist expressed something closely akin to this idea when he said: "No good thing does the Lord withhold from those who walk uprightly" (Psalm 84:11). The Lord does not ask or expect a child of his to give up one single thing that is best for him. God may want and request us to give up many things, but they will be things or activities that will not be best for us.

Why not try an experiment before going on to the "Three Tests" in the next chapter? On the basis of the three major questions in this chapter, decide whether or not it is right for you to participate in a particular activity. Try the questions on some activity about which you have no serious doubt. Then apply them to an activity concerning which you are somewhat doubtful. Some possible activities might be athletics such as football, basketball, baseball, and tennis; amusements such as movies, wrestling matches, and dancing; or more strictly personal matters such as studying on Sunday, flipping a coin for drinks, or petting.

If you get any effective guidance from the use of the questions, remember that you will have to want to know what is right; you will have to search sincerely for the truth.

6

RIGHT OR WRONG:
Three Tests

In these chapters we are seeking to discover principles or methods by which we can know whether or not a particular activity is right or wrong. In the preceding chapter we applied the test of effect—effect upon ourselves, upon others, and upon the cause of Christ. In this chapter we are going to suggest three additional tests. Some of you may find these tests easier to apply than the questions of the preceding chapter. At least, they may be used to supplement the questions.

Let us suggest again that you will be helped to the degree that you sincerely want to be helped and are willing to face up to the challenge presented by the tests.

The Test of Secrecy

Let us imagine that, as you read this, you are in the process of deciding whether it would be right or wrong for you to cheat. Or you might supply another activity that applies especially to you. How can the test of secrecy help you?

The following additional questions may help you answer that question: "Are there some individuals that you would prefer not to know about it if you did that thing?" "What about your mother; would you be embarrassed for her to know?" "What about your father, your Sunday school teacher, your youth leader or counselor, your pastor, your best friend, the best Christian you know: would you prefer for one or more of them not to know?" If you would, will you not agree that you should at least raise a question about your participation in that activity? We are not saying now that it would be right or wrong but simply that it would be questionable.

We can be sure that the right is never afraid of the light. On the other hand, wrong seeks to avoid or to hide itself from the light. It is no mere accident that most crimes are committed at night. It was Jesus who said, "Every one who does evil hates the light, and does not come to the light, lest his deeds should be exposed. But he who does what is true comes to the light, that it may be clearly seen that his deeds have been wrought in God" (John 3:20–21).

Do you remember how you reacted when you were a child and had done something that you knew your mother disapproved? Did you not evade her as much as possible? You were uncomfortable in her presence. This was true not only because you were afraid she might discover what you had done but also because there was an inner something that condemned you. You did not feel at ease in her presence.

Now, what about the activity you were considering? Will it pass the test of secrecy? Would you be willing to bring it into the full light of truth? To make the test more tangible, would it be all right with you, if you went ahead and did this thing, for that fact to be flashed on a screen at your school at chapel time or at a worship service of your church?

We may be able to keep our participation secret from others, but there is one who will know. God, whom we call "Our Father," will know: He sees all; he hears all; he knows all. Would we want him to know?

Test of Universality

This is another simple test that can aid us in times of decision. It will be equally helpful to young people and older people as long as they are honest seekers after truth.

We may understand this test and its significance a little better if we ask some questions. Incidentally, are you keeping in mind the activity or decision you were asked to consider at the first of the chapter? Think about it as we proceed with the discussion.

Some of the questions we might profitably ask ourselves are:

"Would it be all right with me if everyone else did this same thing?" Occasionally, someone in a conference where we discuss these matters answers, "Oh, sure, it would be perfectly all right." One who is inclined to answer in that way should be asked some more specific questions such as the following, which will make the general question more searching: "Would it be all right for your Mom to do it, or your Dad, or your teacher, or your pastor?" "Would you approve their participation?" "Would it be inappropriate for them to do this thing?" "Would you lose a little respect for them if you saw them doing it?"

What if one makes some exceptions and says: "No, I would not expect Mom to do that." "I would be horrified to see my Dad doing it." "I just cannot imagine my pastor participating in it." If one raises questions concerning the participation of any of these, then does not the activity fail to pass the universality test? Should not this fact raise a question concerning one's participation in it? Let us make it very personal. Is there not a considerable possibility that if I react unfavorably to the participation of another in a certain activity, then someone may react in a similar way to my participation?

We should also make a general application of the universality test. Let us ask: "What kind of a family, a church, a community, a world would we have if everybody did this particular thing?" You have possibly seen a slogan on a church wall that asks a searching and legitimate question, which is not only applicable to the church but also to the family and the world. The slogan is: "What kind of a church would my church be, if every member of my church were just like me?"

If we admit that we would have a rather sorry family, church, community, and world if everyone did this thing, then, would that not mean that it would be wrong for us? If, on the other hand, we can honestly say, "We would have a glorious and a better family, church, community, and world if everyone did this thing," then is it not right and wise for us to do it? Every activity of our lives should pass at least the negative test and it would be even better if it passed the positive.

Test of Prayer

There is no higher test for any activity than to ask: "Can I pray about it?" "Can I ask God to go with me?" "Can I ask him to bless me in the doing of it?"

Should not a Christian feel free to pray about anything he does? If he does not consider it appropriate to invite the Lord to go with him or to bless him as he does that particular thing, is that not a good indication that the activity would be unwise or wrong for him?

To pass the test of prayer does not mean necessarily that we will always pray concerning that activity, but it does mean that we could, in good conscience, pray about it. We could feel perfectly at ease talking it over with our Father. Talking with him about it would be normal and natural and would create no strain in our relations.

A number of years ago Charles M. Sheldon wrote a book, which became a best seller, entitled *In His Steps*. It continues to be rather widely read. If you have not read it, I would suggest that you do so. In that book the author recommends that the Christian, at every time of decision, should ask, "What would Jesus do?" That is a good and searching question.

Some people, however, have criticized Sheldon's book and particularly his central emphasis, saying that it is an over-simplification of the problems of life. Some have suggested that a more proper and helpful question would be: "What would Jesus have me to do?" They contend that Jesus was God as well as man and that he lived a perfect life, which we cannot do. Both of the questions, it seems to me, can be practically equated with the test of prayer.

Incidentally, there may not be as much difference in those two questions as some would have us think. You will remember that Paul said: "Be imitators of me, as I am of Christ" (1 Cor. 11:1). If Paul followed Christ—and he did—was it not natural for him to counsel the Corinthian Christians and us to follow Christ? Also, it is possible that in most, if not all, situations of life Jesus would have us do what he would do under similar circumstances. But whether we think it should be "What would Jesus do?" or "What would Jesus have me to do?" certainly we will agree that we should ask the question or questions, and that they will probe rather deeply.

Possibly some of you are saying, "There is nothing that will pass such a high test. To live life on such a high level would take all the joy out of living." Surely, you do not really believe that. There are many activities that will pass the test of prayer, as well as the preceding tests.

For example, I know a man who played football seven years. He was not a Christian during the first two years of high school. His sister testified that during that time he never played a game that she did not pray for him.

He says that from the time he was converted until he had played out his string in college he never played a game that he did not first talk to the Lord about it. He asked the Lord to bless him and his teammates, to help them to play hard and clean, and to help those who were Christians, in some way, even in the midst of the game, to reveal the true Christian spirit.

There are many other activities that will pass all three tests. Let us also remember that if an activity will not pass them, it will not be best for us.

Conclusion

Have you followed through on the suggestion at the first of this chapter that you apply these tests to some particular activity? If you have not, why not try an experiment similar to the one suggested at the close of the preceding chapter? Select some activity about which you must make a decision and consistently apply these tests. See what the result will be. Do not be afraid to do it. It may be a very rewarding experience. The Lord will help you if you will ask sincerely for his guidance and wisdom.

Some might complain that the application of these tests will take the joy out of life. In answer, we can state that, instead of lessening, the joy will be increased and enriched even in the field of play and recreation. We should not close this chapter, however, without a few words concerning the deeper joy of a Christian.

The Christians with the most abiding joy and peace in their hearts—a peace and a joy that passes understanding, that cannot be disturbed by external conditions—are those who have a sense of the abiding presence of God. They have a deep conviction of being within his will. Anything that will not pass the high tests we have suggested will sooner or later destroy the very happiness and joy we desire. God's good men and women, his obedient sons and daughters, are his happiest people.

Someone has rather wisely said that most Christians have just enough religion to make them miserable. They have enough that they are uncomfortable in sin; they do not have enough to keep them from sin. The only ones who ever tap the depths of the blessings that are in God are those who have the courage and the strength of character to sacrifice the lower things of life. Life on the higher levels is reserved for those who sacrifice it on the lower levels. Where do we want to live: on the mountains or high planes of vision, of challenge, and of service or in the valleys of darkness, despondency, and defeat? Right now, you may be in the process of deciding. Something that may seem to be a minor decision may set the direction of your life for the indefinite future. That is what makes every decision potentially a major one.

Do not forget that Satan may seem to have some happy young people, but he does not have any happy old people. Is it not fair to say that even Satan's young people have a deep dissatisfaction and a hunger for a more meaningful and happier life? It will always be wise to take the deep look and the long look in any time of decision, however insignificant the decision may seem to be.

7

RIGHT OR WRONG:
Three Sources of Light

In the last two chapters we have given attention to some specific questions or tests that may help us to decide what is right or wrong when we are faced with an immediate decision. To supplement the last two chapters, we want to suggest three sources of light that are available to the Christian.

LIGHT FROM WITHIN

This chapter, as was true of the last two, will be more practical and helpful if you will keep in mind some particular activity or problem. Attempt to determine whether that activity is right or wrong, wise or unwise.

One source of light in a time of decision is the light from within ourselves. God has created us with certain innate or inborn powers. If we are normal enough to be morally responsible, we have the power to think, to reason, to judge, to evaluate, to will. We also possess, as a part of our native equipment, a sense of oughtness or a conviction or feeling that there is such a thing as right and wrong.

God, who knows what is best for us, has put the responsibility squarely upon us to determine for ourselves what is right and wrong for us to do. It is understood that, while we are immature, this responsibility is shared by our parents, teachers, and others. The ultimate goal, however, of all moral and spiritual teaching and training is that the individual may reach full maturity. This, in turn, means that he will have the equipment with which to make wise decisions, which likewise means that he will have full responsibility for what he does.

God, who has given to man a native capacity for moral living, expects man to accept the responsibilities that such ability or capacity entails. This means that even during the maturing process, God expects us to use every inner resource we have to determine for ourselves what is right and wrong. He is not going to reveal, in some miraculous way, his will to us without our cooperation.

When faced with a particular decision, we should think through every possible angle of the problem. As suggested previously, we should weigh, as objectively as possible, its total effects on us, on others, and on the cause of Christ. The tests, discussed in the preceding chapters, should be fearlessly applied. The sincere use of the resources we have will be so blessed by the Lord as to give us the sense of divine guidance that we need. The matter may be summed up as follows: When one is faced with a decision concerning right or wrong, there is no substitute for consecrated common sense.

When we have a sense of the direction in which we should go, the response to that feeling is an inner, personal one. In other words, God gives to us the power of decision. We can say "Yes" or "No" to the light that comes. God will not override our wills. But we should never forget that the freedom to choose carries with it the responsibility for the choice.

LIGHT FROM WITHOUT

In a time of decision we may not only receive light from within, but we may receive considerable help from without if we have eyes that see, ears that hear, minds that interpret, and wills that respond to the light that comes.

By "light from without" we mean, among other things, the aid we can receive from others, particularly those who are older, more experienced, or morally and spiritually more mature. These more mature individuals have faced similar decisions. They know, through observation and experience, the ultimate results of certain lines of conduct. They usually have the advantage of a broader perspective and a deeper insight into life and its problems than those who are more immature.

It is hoped that this will not encourage you to be too dependent upon others. As you mature—and you are in the process now —you increasingly should make up your own mind. This, in turn, does not mean that you should assert a premature independence. It does mean, however, that you should be willing to accept the responsibilities of the maturing process.

On the other hand, we should remember, regardless of how mature we may be, that we can be helped by others. No one of us has all the light he needs for many of the decisions of life. Even the light we have has come, to a considerable degree, from parents and others who have shaped our thinking and who have built into our lives basic moral ideas and ideals.

Our parents, teachers, leaders, pastors, and others, who have had much more experience than we have had, would like to save us from many mistakes. This does not mean that we should seek, on every occasion of decision, to advise with any one or all of them. We do not want to develop a neurotic sense of dependence on others. We do not want to become "counselor addicts"; those who seek counsel from every counselor who comes along.

Much of the soundest counsel we shall receive from parents, teachers, leaders, pastors, and other adults, will come to us as we listen to them in the home, the classroom, or the church. Some of it will come through formal instruction; much of it will be gathered from casual conversation. The latter rather than the former frequently is more revealing of the motivating principles of one's life, and hence it is often more influential in the lives of those who are touched by it.

This does not mean that we should not seek the help of parents and adult friends when we really need it. This we can and should do, admitting frankly our limitations and our need for additional light. Let us not forget in such times that we have sought counsel from that particular individual because we believe he is more mature than we are. We also have confidence in his basic integrity and his genuine interest in us.

As a result of our confidence in the one from whom we have sought the advice, we certainly will give serious consideration to any light we receive from him. This should be true, in particular, of the counsel received from parents. Parents, with rare exceptions, are more interested in us and in our welfare than anyone else. They would like to use the light that has come to them, as they have traveled life's pathway, to light our pathway and to save us from some of the errors they have made along the way.

You may be disappointed at times that the adults from whom you seek advice do not give you more positive guidance. In most cases this is done deliberately. The wise counselor hopes to lead you to make your own decision with as little suggestion or direction from him as necessary. He wants to shed the light that will help you to see the way you should go. He wants you to discover for yourself as much of that light as possible. He then hopes that you will make your own decision without a positive recommendation from him. If he can succeed in leading you to such a personal decision, he knows that it will be more meaningful to you than a decision you make at his suggestion.

There is another source of light from without that would save many young people from tragic mistakes if they would keep their eyes and ears open and their minds alert. The light we are referring to is that which comes to us by observing, in the lives of others, the ultimate results of particular lines of conduct.

For example, if we are trying to decide whether it is right or wrong for us to smoke, to gamble, to drink, to pet, to dance, let us observe what the results are in the lives of those who participate in such activities. Let us watch for the more immediate as well as the final results. What about some of our acquaintances: did we notice any good or bad effects in them when they began to participate in one or more of these activities? What about the effects on their personalities? What about their appreciation for the finer things of life? What seemed to be the effect on their relation to their church and their Lord?

However, to see the full picture and hence to judge the results fairly, we must look beyond the high school or the college campus if we want to see the ultimate results. We even must study the influence of one's participation in a particular activity on the home and on society in general. We should visit the slums and jails of our cities.

On one such visit, the police captain said that he was sure the police department had arrested "Aunt Mary" at least 700 times for drunkenness. He reported that there was a time when she was a highly respected woman in the community. She had become a slave to drink, as is true of hundreds of thousands of other men and women. What a contrast between "Aunt Mary" and the beautiful advertisements in the magazines and the attractive posters on the billboards. "Aunt Mary" would considerably mar those pictures, but she belongs in them if they are going to be accurate. Young people need to see "Aunt Mary" in those pictures. If they did, she would help them to know what to do about drinking.

This is merely one illustration of what is meant by the light from without. Intelligent observation will save us from many mistakes.

LIGHT FROM ABOVE

This is another source of light, available to all children of God. We can and should utilize it in times of decision. Let us suggest again that the Lord expects us to use the resources we have to choose the right and to refuse the wrong. This is different, however, from saying that we have, within ourselves, all the resources we need for life's decisions. An important step in any wise decision concerning a major problem is a proper sense of our own limitations. We should acknowledge that we cannot think as clearly as we should unless we have the leadership of the Holy Spirit. We should admit our need for the Lord's guidance and should seek that guidance even as we use every resource available to us in an attempt to determine what is right or wrong.

In other words, as we ask the questions, as we make the tests suggested in preceding chapters, we should do so in the spirit of prayer. Also, as we seek the counsel and advice of others, we should ask the Spirit of God to lead them and us.

Even when we have sought as prayerfully as we know how all the light possible from within and from without, we may still be in doubt. At such times, let us call to mind what James says: "If any of you lacks wisdom, let him ask God who gives to all generously and without reproaching; and it will be given him" (James 1:5).

An important source for the light that comes from above is the Bible. The Bible is not a rule book, but wherever it does speak specifically it is authoritative. We will find in the Bible basic principles that will provide the foundation for wise Christian choices. If we saturate ourselves in its spirit, if we build its ideals into our lives, we shall have the moral and spiritual alertness that is needed for us to choose wisely.

In response to our prayers, our Bible study, and our sincere seeking, God may not flood our souls with light, but he will give us enough light to take the next step. Let us follow whatever light we have, although it may not be more than a gleam, with complete confidence that God will give us additional light as it is needed. This will be true in regard to the problems we are going to discuss in Part II. It also can be and will be true, if we will do our part, in regard to other decisions we shall make as we journey life's pathway.

Many times the most serious problem arises after we know what we ought to do. We seem to lack the will power to make ourselves do what we know we should do. It is then that we need the help of the One "who in every respect has been tempted as we are yet without sinning," and we can draw near to him in confidence knowing that we will "receive mercy and grace in time of need" (Heb. 4:15–16).

Part II

PROBLEMS

8

PRINCIPLES AND PRACTICE

The chapters of Part I have dealt with principles of Christian conduct. They have been written with the hope and prayer that they will be helpful to you. I trust you have not by-passed those chapters. I consider them more basically important than the chapters of this section dealing with specific problems. If you accept the principles, apply them honestly, and utilize the sources of help suggested, you can be trusted, to a large degree, to decide for yourself what is right and wrong for you to do.

In the chapters in Part II we shall attempt to apply those general principles to some of the more prevalent problems among young people. Naturally, we cannot review all the pertinent principles in connection with each problem. It is hoped that you will study these chapters deliberately and slowly enough to review and to apply the basic principles, including the questions and tests suggested.

A REVIEW OF THE PRINCIPLES

Before we proceed to a discussion of specific problems, it may be of some value to review some of the more significant conclusions or principles of Part I. They are as follows:

(1) While all of us live, to a certain degree, on the instinctive, the customary, and the conscience levels, the level on which a Christian should live is the distinctly Christian level (Chapter I).

(2) The Christian is not his own. He—his body, his mind, his total personality—belongs to God, but God has seen fit to make him a steward. Being a slave and a steward, all he has of material goods, of time, and of talents, belongs to God and is to be used

under the direction of God to serve God and his fellow man (Chapter II).

(3) Some things are wrong within themselves, while other activities are made unwise or wrong for us because of the environment in which they are usually found or the attitude of others toward our participation in them (Chapter III).

(4) The final source of authority for man is not within himself or within the social group or community to which he belongs, but it is the will of God, which man can know and which he will discover is always best for him (Chapter IV).

(5) When we are faced with a decision involving right or wrong, we can find help by asking three questions: how will my participation in this activity affect me, others, and the cause of Christ (Chapter V); by making three simple tests: the test of secrecy, the test of universality, and the test of prayer (Chapter VI); and by utilizing three sources of light: the light from within, the light from without, and the light from above (Chapter VII). These questions, these tests, these sources of light are not only methods by which we can know the right and the wrong, but they also contain some fundamental principles that we can use in making our decisions.

IMPORTANCE OF THE PRINCIPLES

As you have read the chapters and as you have reviewed the principles, have you thought through and understood them? A more important question is: "Do you accept them as valid for a Christian?"

Whether or not you agree with the principles outlined in the preceding chapters, it is very important for you to have a hard core of Christian principles which will provide you with a base of operation. Before long, if not at the present time, you are going to be on your own. Every decision will be yours to make. Blessed is the young person who is prepared for that day. An essential part of the preparation is the formulation of a Christian philosophy of life, a philosophy that is built upon sound Christian principles.

Certainly, I would like to think that every one of you will agree
with me concerning the problems we shall discuss in Part II.
Doubtless that will not be true. Let me say frankly that I am
much more interested in your acceptance of the basic principles
of Part I. My viewpoint is that if you have a sound basis for the
decisions of life and honestly search for the right, then as you
mature you will finally, if not immediately, arrive at the right
position concerning most if not all of the problems and decisions
you will face.

One of my chief concerns is that you will think carefully
through every problem or decision. I would rather for you to
think and disagree with me than to agree and not think.

My main concern, however, is that you be honest in your
search for what is right and wrong. I know if that is true, then
God will give you guidance and assurance and will not permit
you to go very far astray. The searching mind and the willing
heart will know what is right and wrong. We should remember
that this searching is a lifetime job. It will be most unfortunate
if we conclude that we have all the knowledge and light we need
concerning any of the problems of life. God himself cannot lead
a closed mind. He reveals additional light to those who set their
faces toward the open road. Principles may be fixed and secure;
an understanding and the application of them is a continuing
process.

Change in Approach

In this section dealing with specific areas of decision, I have
found it advisable to change my approach to some degree. In
line with the preceding viewpoint, you will find a more frequent
use of questions and less often a statement of a positive position,
although I will not hesitate to make the latter when it seems
wise or necessary to do so.

This change in approach and emphasis has been made deliberately. One reason for the change is that I want you to apply for
yourself the basic principles to the specific problems considered.
I want you to answer for yourself the question: "Is this activity

right or wrong for me as a Christian?" It is far more important for you to be led to make a wise, personal decision than for you to understand or to agree with my position. I do not think you will have much difficulty knowing my position.

If you think through to a clear-cut, defensible Christian position on all the problems, you must take time to deliberate, to meditate, and to pray. It is hoped that you will be willing to give whatever time is necessary. There is a possibility that a decision concerning your relation to one of these activities may be the most important decision you face at this particular time. A right decision in regard to that problem may provide the basis for many other wise decisions in the years to come.

You possibly have already observed another change in approach. In these chapters dealing with specific problems, I have found it advisable and necessary to change, to some degree, my use of pronouns. I shall use "we" less and "I" and "you" more.

In the section dealing with principles, I could properly use "we." The principles suggested are just as valid for me today as when I was your age. In contrast, my positions concerning most of the problems discussed in Part II were established years ago. I do not mean that I have a closed mind concerning these matters, but for me, with one or two possible exceptions, these are no longer problems. I do not have to argue with myself or reason within myself whether or not these things are right or wrong for me to do.

Do not forget, however, that I once faced the same decisions that many of you are in the process of making. Also, through the years I have been interested in young people and have given much time to personal and group conferences with them concerning these problems. Try, as best you can, to think of these chapters as personal chats with you or as conferences with a group of Christian youth.

9

CHEATING

You have doubtless discovered by now that being a real Christian is a practical, down-to-earth, everyday affair. It involves what we are on Monday as well as what we are on Sunday; what we do on the playground, on the bus, and in the classroom as well as what we do in the church or in the church organizations. This means that whether or not one cheats is a Christian decision.

What has been your observation; is cheating prevalent in your school or college? Do Christian students as well as non-Christians cheat?

Questionnaires filled out by forty-six student secretaries on college campuses revealed that only two of them said that there was no cheating on their campuses. One of those campuses was a state university and the other a privately endowed institution, both of them having, so it was stated, an effective honor system.

In contrast, four secretaries suggested that 50 per cent or more of the students were involved in the practice, with an additional sixteen estimating that 25 to 50 per cent of the students cheated. Unfair work on papers and other assignments was even more prevalent.

Do you know conscientious Christian young people who are disturbed about cheating, either because of its prevalence among their fellow students or because of their own involvement in it? Has it become a rather acute problem for some of them?

DEFINITION OF CHEATING

Before we specifically examine the rightness or wrongness of cheating, it may be of some value to consider its meaning. We may discover that it is more inclusive than we usually have thought. This, in turn, may cause some of us to search our lives a little more carefully to see if we are cheating, although we may not cheat on tests and examinations.

At least occasionally a dictionary definition is of some value. The definition of "cheat" in *Webster's Dictionary of Synonyms* is as follows: "Cheat suggests deceit and, usually, tricks that escape or are intended to escape the observation of others." Words closely related to cheat are listed, such as defraud, dupe, delude, swindle, double-cross, hoodwink, bamboozle, and mislead. Those words, to varying degrees, carry a bad meaning or connotation.

When cheating is thus defined, will you not agree that it is considerably broader or more comprehensive than most people think? In a sense, it includes everything we do to deceive, to trick, or to defraud. It embraces unfair work on classroom assignments just as definitely as it includes unfair work on tests and examinations.

One can also cheat on the athletic field, at the corner drug store, or in his day-by-day relations with others. An employee who does not give an honest day or an honest hour's work is cheating. An employer who withholds that which rightfully belongs to his employee is cheating. Similarly, parents can cheat children and children can cheat parents by duping or deceiving each other. When it is understood properly, we see that cheating reaches into most areas of life.

DEFENSE OF CHEATING

In the remainder of our discussion we shall restrict ourselves to cheating in the classroom, which is possibly the area most familiar to you and the realm in which you are most immediately interested. What defenses are given most frequently for cheating?

Have you observed that one of the most common defenses is: "Everyone else cheats." The implication is: "Why shouldn't I?"

What has been your experience: does everyone cheat? Do you know Christian young people, and even some who do not claim to be Christians, who do not cheat? Is one who gives this reason for cheating usually doing so to justify his own cheating? The psychologists call such a process rationalization.

I will concede, and I judge you will admit, that the pressure in some schools is terrific for one to cheat. In one sense such pressure or testing may be good for the Christian student. One does not develop strong Christian character in a moral vacuum. He grows it by facing the temptations of life and having the victory over them.

Where is the Christian supposed to get his standards of right and wrong: from the crowd or from his own honest convictions as to what he considers to be right and wrong for him as a child of God? Will you not agree that he should do what he considers to be right regardless of what others may think or do? This he will do if he is dead serious about being a real Christian and if he makes God's will the supreme source of authority in his life.

"Teachers are unfair," is another defense sometimes given for cheating. What do you think about the charge? Is it just? Are most teachers fair or unfair?

As a teacher I will admit that some teachers give unfair assignments and, occasionally, they may give an unfair examination. It is also true that there tends to be too much of a spirit of competition rather than co-operation between teachers and students.

What if a teacher is unfair, which I am persuaded is rare? Will that fact make it right for a student to cheat? Will two wrongs ever make a thing right?

There are other students who say "Nobody cares," and they include their teachers in "nobody." Unfortunately, there are some teachers who do not seem to be concerned very much about cheating. Many of one's fellow students may not care. But is it true that no one cares? What about father, mother, Sunday school teacher, and pastor—do they care? Are there not some students disappointed and, to some degree, disillusioned when they see a Christian cheat? Does Jesus care?

There are still others who say "Cheating is the only way I can make my grades." They may mean they cannot pass without cheating. Is that very often true? Or, they may mean that they cannot maintain as high a grade level as they want without cheating. Do those who cheat ordinarily make better grades than those who do not cheat? Even if one could not pass without cheating, which is more honorable and more Christian: to fail honestly or to fail to be honest?

COUNTS AGAINST CHEATING

What do you think of the preceding and other defenses that are made of cheating? Does any one or do all of them justify a Christian cheating? Is cheating right or wrong? What are some of the chief counts against it?

One of the main counts against cheating is the fact that the cheater cheats himself. The one who cheats may receive a grade he does not deserve from the teacher. He may and does cheat his fellow students. But the main one who is hurt is the cheater himself.

Think of the different ways he cheats himself. He cheats himself of knowledge that would be his through honest effort. He deprives himself of good study habits; habits that would be an asset to him through the years. He will lack the sharpening and development of his mind that comes as a result of the mastery of a stiff assignment or the conquest of a difficult problem. Also, cheating may lead to lying and other forms of deception and to dishonesty in other relationships of life.

The cheater may discover that his moral sensitivities will be dulled. This will be true if down deep he considers cheating wrong. When one does a thing his better self says is wrong, he seeks to find a way to justify himself. When he justifies himself, he tends to twist his moral judgment in such a way that it can no longer be trusted. His soul tends to be warped.

Do you remember the second question in Chapter V? It was "How will my participation in this activity affect others?" What about cheating? Will it pass the test of this question? Is it true that when one cheats, he cheats not only himself but he is unfair to his fellow students who are honest? But what about the influence of his cheating, if he is a Christian, upon other students:

those who are Christians but particularly the non-Christians?

Two college freshmen were roommates: one a Christian, the other a non-Christian. The non-Christian came in one day bitterly denouncing a fellow student whom he had seen cheating. He did not have any personal scruples against cheating, but the student he had seen cheating was one of the "religious students" of the campus. Most non-Christians expect Christians to maintain higher standards than they do. Should we not count this a compliment to the Christian religion, and should we not seek to live on a level that will not disappoint our unsaved friends and neighbors?

The following additional questions may help you to decide on the rightness or wrongness of cheating: What would be the effect on your school if everybody cheated? Would it be a better school if no one cheated? Can you think of a single vocation or profession in which cheating in school would be considered a good recommendation for an applicant for a position? Is cheating an asset or a liability to one?

Conclusions Concerning Cheating

In addition to the above, make the three tests (Chapter VI) and utilize the three sources of light (Chapter VII). Will cheating stand up under the light that is revealed? For example, can cheating pass the test of secrecy, of universality, of prayer? It cannot and never could pass those tests for me. Can it pass them for you?

Do you believe cheating is one activity that is wrong within itself? If it is, then it can never be made right because of the attitude of others toward it. And we can be sure that one who cheats will pay a price for cheating. He may never be caught by his teacher or even by his fellow students, but he cannot escape his own best self. He will pay a price for his cheating, at least in his own mind and soul.

If cheating is wrong, then it, like any other sin, will separate one from God. We can never escape the searching eye of God.

If you have been cheating, will you honestly and prayerfully search your own soul and arrive at a definite conclusion concerning it, a conclusion that will be Christ honoring? May the Lord give you the necessary grace and courage to make the right decision.

Doubtless many of you Christian young people do not cheat and you have felt that this chapter has not applied to you. I dare say, however, that some of you have been under considerable pressure to give aid to some one else. It is possible that the giving of such aid is considered a test of friendship on your campus. One can become very unpopular by refusing to help a fellow student. What do you think a Christian student should do when he is asked for assistance on a test or an examination or when he is asked to give unfair help on an outside assignment? Do you know what one is called who has rendered aid to another person who has committed a crime? Such a one is said to be a *particeps criminis* or an accomplice, although he did not actively participate in the crime. If proved guilty, he can be sent to prison. Does assisting one in cheating or doing unfair work make the one giving the assistance a *particeps criminis?*

"An honest man's the noblest work of God."—Pope.

$$\boxed{10}$$

GAMBLING

I was in Cincinnati and had a couple of hours before I was to catch a night train. While taking a walk to get some fresh air, I noticed a constant stream of people entering a parochial school building. I decided to join the crowd and see what was happening inside.

It was bingo night, a weekly feature, under the auspices of the church and the school. I was permitted to roam around. People were crowded into every nook and cranny of the school building. All the classrooms were filled, and the auditorium—even the platform—was full of players. Tables and players were found in some of the halls. There were 1,500 to 2,000 people present, each of whom had paid $1.00 for a bingo card. Soft drinks and beer were being sold. Winners and prizes were announced over the public address system. The profits, I was told, went to the church and the school.

I assume that most of you have a conviction against gambling, and would label what these people, under the auspices of the church, were doing as gambling. But there are other activities concerning which you may not be so sure. It may be that something that is said in this chapter will help you to determine when an activity is gambling and when it involves only the necessary and legitimate risk or chance element.

PREVALENCE OF GAMBLING

Just a casual reading of the newspapers and news magazines will reveal how widespread gambling is among young people and adults. It has been estimated by one of the leading students of gambling that fifty million adult Americans gamble regularly, "butting their heads and dollars against gambling odds and gimmicks that make it impossible for them to win." [1]

Other figures gathered from the same article and other articles in *The Annals,* May, 1950, disclose that twenty-six million Americans play bingo, which is "just as much a gambling game as lottery," with about twenty-two million playing dice or cards for money, nineteen million betting on athletic events and eight million on the horses each year. During a recent year, the latter group bet over $1,600,000,000 through the pari-mutuel machines, with an additional $8,000,000,000 bet by individuals through bookmakers.

There are fourteen million slot-machine addicts who "wage a perpetual losing battle with the one-armed bandits." If one will add to the preceding the people who play the numbers game, buy tickets for the Irish sweepstakes, purchase a chance on an auto or a trip to the Bahamas, toss the rings or the coins or spin the wheel at the carnivals, or participate in football or baseball pools, he can begin to see how widely gambling is practiced by the American people.

DEFENSE OF GAMBLING

Some defend gambling by saying that it is natural. They contend that it expresses an inborn tendency and that one should express and not repress his natural urges. It is doubtful if a very strong case can be made for gambling as an expression of an innate urge or hunger.

Let us assume, however, that it results, to a degree, from man's desire to take chances. Is there not a difference between a natural urge to take a chance and the desire to gamble? Can these two be equated? Is not gambling merely one way to express the desire, innate or otherwise, to take a chance? One thing that distinguishes gambling from the legitimate chances we all have to take is the fact that what one man wins or gains from gambling an-

---

[1] Blanche, Ernest E., "Gambling Odds Are Gimmicked!," *The Annals of The American Academy of Political and Social Science,* May 1950. This entire volume of *The Annals* is on gambling.

other loses, or at least he does not gain anything from the experience.

Also, while it will be conceded that no innate hunger of man is wrong within itself, yet every hunger or urge of man can be expressed in wrong ways, in ways that will hurt him, others, and society. The latter is just as true of the urge to take a chance, assuming that it is innate, as it is of the desire for food or drink.

One of the most common defenses of gambling is the insistence that life itself is a gamble. It is argued that the business man gambles on the fluctuation of prices, the farmer on the weather, the pedestrian on the auto driver, and the insurance companies on all of us.

All of life is a gamble, so it is argued. Parents gamble on their children. Young people gamble when they establish a new home. Getting an education is a gamble: We cannot know what tomorrow will bring; we do not know that we shall use our education; we cannot be sure that we shall be suited for the work for which we are preparing ourselves. The implication is that since the chance element is so common to all of life, gambling is not wrong. It is merely another expression of this risk element.

Is there not considerable difference, however, between taking the ordinary chances of life and gambling? Do we not in the regular processes of life seek to reduce the risk or chance element to the minimum? Is this not true of the business man or the farmer and of the intelligent young person as he prepares for his life's work or as he chooses his life's companion?

On the other hand, gambling does not seek to eliminate and does little to reduce the risk element. It could not exist without that element. There is, however, one group involved in gambling who not only attempt but actually do eliminate chance in gambling, so far as they are concerned. They are the operators who live by gambling. They have worked out and control the odds so they always win. Those who patronize or gamble with them take the risks and the losses.

There are some people who attempt to defend gambling, as they do many other practices, by claiming that it is a purely per-

sonal matter. They contend that each individual should be free
to do as he pleases about it, that it should be no one else's business. But can gambling be so defended? Does not the one who
gambles inevitably involve one or more other persons? Are the
effects strictly personal? Does not gambling affect friends, neighbors, loved ones, and the community as a whole? "No man gam-
bleth unto himself." Since this is true, may it not be somebody's
business and society's business what one does about gambling?

"YOU CAN'T WIN"

This is the title of a book on gambling by Ernest E. Blanche,
the chief statistician for the Logistic Division of the Army General Staff, who approaches the study of gambling from the mathematical viewpoint.[2] In this book and in his article and in the
other articles in *The Annals,* mentioned previously, there is
enough evidence to prove that any person who gambles is not
exercising good common sense.

"The mathematical probabilities are always against the bet-
tor." There is an old saying that horse players always die broke.
That is not only true of horse players but of most others who are
possessed by the gambling habit. From the personal material
viewpoint, gambling does not pay.

What about forms of gambling that are a little closer to young
people? Blanche concludes, based on his own careful investiga-
tions, that carnival games, with an occasional exception, are de-
signed or "fixed" so the operators can be sure to get from 50 to
90 per cent of all the money spent or wagered.

The fact that pinball machines are called "one-armed bandits"
suggests that a player cannot beat them. Blanche says, "Every
machine I have ever examined has been 'fixed' to pay off only a
small percentage of the money taken in. Usually the machine is
adjusted to give back from 10 to 20 per cent of the money put
into the slot." An anonymous writer in *The Annals* says "No
other machine was ever invented from which the profits derived

[2] The subtitle of his book is "Facts and Fallacies About Gambling,"
Washington: Public Affairs Press, 1949.

were so fabulous on so small an investment, and with so little effort."

THE EFFECTS OF GAMBLING

Plain common sense should keep one from gambling. When one recognizes that he cannot win, should he not be convinced that gambling is unwise for any person—Christian or non-Christian?

Such a utilitarian or common sense approach to gambling is not, however, the final or strongest argument against it. Some people might and do say, "I know all of that, but I want to gamble anyway. I enjoy it. Is there any difference between my spending my money to gamble and you spending yours for a ticket to the opera or to the football game? It is my form of recreation. You can have yours; let me have mine."

There is a difference, and we can see that difference if we will observe the effects of gambling on the individual and on society. Gambling seems to be habit forming. Some people have a constitutional weakness for it just as some have for alcohol. It demands more and more if the desire is to be satisfied. It gets such a grip on some people that they seemingly cannot break the habit. Frequently, they gamble with the money they should use for family necessities, and some even steal to cover up their losses.

Some years ago in California an organization was started known as Gamblers Anonymous, patterned after Alcoholics Anonymous. Starting with a membership of twenty-one, they now number their members in the thousands. Their purpose is to help each other to break the gambling habit.

Gambling taints or leaves a stain on everybody and everything it touches. "Dishonesty and fraud have always been integral parts of the gambling business." It threatens collegiate and professional athletics. The college basketball scandals of recent years are evidence of this fact. Gambling corrupts communities and nations. It is like a leech fastened on the social order. Politicians are frequently its slaves and protectors. Even "the slot machine has . . . become a threat to good government." What one writer says concerning lotteries could be said concerning all forms of gambling: "Lotteries change the very pattern of living, distort the sense of values, and incubate the eggs of crime."

No wonder one writer concludes: "The business of gambling is entirely parasitic, and exists for the sole purpose of exploiting a human weakness." Is it not common sense that we should not surrender to that human weakness, that we should not be a contributor to a business so damaging to individuals and to society?

CONCLUSION

What is your conclusion concerning gambling? In an earlier chapter we suggested that some things were wrong because of the environment in which they were usually found or because of the attitude of others toward those activities. It was also stated that there are some things wrong within themselves. In which of these categories does gambling belong? It may belong, in one sense, in all of them, but is it not wrong basically because it is wrong within itself?

You will remember we suggested that an activity which was wrong within itself could never be right regardless of the attitude of others toward it. If gambling is inherently wrong, then it can never be right for one to participate in it, although all others were doing so and even the community as such approved it. This would mean that gambling would still be wrong even if sponsored by a humanitarian or religious institution and the proceeds went to worthy objects.

This position will put our relation to gambling above the customary level and will raise it to the Christian one. Anything that is inherently wrong certainly should be recognized as contrary to the will of God, and God's will is the final source of authority for the Christian in the area of right and wrong. This means that we should avoid all forms of gambling, even the simplest and least expensive.

One of the strongest arguments against gambling, even the simplest forms, is the fact that it feeds upon and in turn contributes to the desire to get something for nothing. This attitude or desire is damaging to character. It is possible that this is the very heart of the gambling problem. If so, then flipping a coin for drinks is basically just as wrong as betting on a football game or shooting craps. Anything that is hurtful to man, who is made in the image of God, is wrong for man.

11

MOVIES

Your immediate reaction may be that everyone attends the movies; why raise any question concerning the Christian and the movies? There are, however, some Christians who do not attend them and do not believe other Christians should attend. There are also some communities where there is considerable sentiment against Christians attending the movies. Then, it may be helpful for us to re-examine our position concerning the matter.

INTRODUCTORY STATEMENTS

The motion picture is one of America's most important educational instruments.

It is possible that the movies, along with television which is a home version of motion pictures, does more to determine the tastes, the values, and the ideals of the American people than any other agency or institution.

The influence of the movies is due, to some degree, to the fact that it reaches so many people. The latest available report reveals a weekly attendance of 65 million, which is a decrease from 80 million in 1946. It is possible that the rapid development of the television field is a factor in this decline. But even 65 millions in one week is quite a crowd.

It is also possible that the industry will soon recapture its clientele with the spread of community theaters and the rapid increase in the number of drive-ins. A book copyrighted in 1939 said there were at that time about a dozen drive-in theaters in the entire country. Eleven now carry advertisements in my daily paper.

Another reason for the marked influence of the movies on those who attend them is the fact that it uses the eye gate. There is no more effective entrance into the mind of man than through the eye. The increasing use of movies in all types of educational processes is an indication of the value placed on the motion picture as an educational instrument.

Of the total weekly attendance, at least 9 million are children who go on Saturday afternoon. They are at a very impressionable period of their lives. The movies have an unusually strong appeal for children and young people. This is another reason for their tremendous influence.

While it is true that the motion picture is one of America's most important educational instruments, its influence, in the main, has been and is bad. Some people possibly have overemphasized the evil effects of the movies, but there is considerable evidence that they have contributed to an increase in juvenile delinquency, to the prevalent idea of bogus romance, to a general distorting of values, and to a lowering of moral standards. Jimmie Fidler, in an article in *Christian Herald,* January, 1949, said: "The motion picture has become America's ace liquor salesman." It is also America's ace salesman for many other things that are bad for America and her people. The industry itself is in such bad repute that a congressional committee was appointed a few years ago to investigate moral conditions among Hollywood's actors and actresses with a threat of national censorship.

Does this mean that the movies are all bad or that they are wrong within themselves? What do you think? Remember that it was suggested earlier that some things are wrong within themselves, while others may be made wrong for one because of the environment in which those things are usually found or because of the attitude of others toward one's participation in them.

Although the influence of motion pictures, in the main, has been bad, movies are not wrong as such or within themselves. This is a personal conclusion. You have a perfect right to disagree. I shall outline, however, some reasons for this position.

There is nothing wrong with the screen, the projector, or the reel. They are merely mechanical instruments. They may be used for good or bad purposes. What makes attendance at a picture show right or wrong is primarily what it does to those who see it. There are other important things that should be considered, as we shall see.

If movies were wrong in themselves, then public schools and churches would be doing wrong when they use them for recreational and educational purposes; denominational boards and agencies would be doing wrong when they produce visual aids including motion pictures; and it would be wrong for one to attend a movie in a school or a church and possibly to watch a television show in a home. Do not conclude from this, however, that it is never wrong for a Christian to attend a movie at a commercial theater. We shall see later that attendance under certain conditions may be very definitely wrong for a Christian.

CURRENT VIEWS

There are at least three rather clearly defined views concerning a Christian's relation to the movies.

"Go when you want to and can."

This doubtless would express, even among Christians, the most prevalent attitude toward motion picture attendance. One who defends this attitude usually says that he goes to the show for recreation, that he is limited as to when he can go, and hence he thinks he is justified in going any time he can and wants to. He argues that seeing a movie is like reading a book. One seldom, if ever, reads a book with which he agrees entirely. He trains himself to accept the true and to reject the false. So it is, he says, with movies. One sees the bad with the good. He can refuse and condemn the bad, while receiving and approving the good. He does not have to let the bad affect him. Is it that simple?

We are not going to take the time or space to evaluate this position. I am confident that most of you do not agree with it.

"Attend only carefully selected shows."

This expresses the attitude of many sincere, consecrated Christians. They suggest that the Christian should select, as wisely as possible, the pictures he attends. This does not mean necessarily that he will approve every detail of the pictures, just as he does not approve everything in the books he reads. As far as possible, however, he will avoid those pictures that will build into his life ideas and ideals contrary to the Christian conception of life.

He may seek help for his selection from trusted Christian friends, from magazines such as *Parents' Magazine* or *Christian Herald,* but he will recognize that he is personally responsible for his choices.

"Do not attend at all."

There also are many consecrated Christians who maintain this position. They do not attend, and they think other Christians should not attend the movies. They contend that the motion picture industry is corrupt from top to bottom, that most of the people who make the pictures are wicked and immoral, and that the total effects of the motion picture business are harmful to individuals and to society.

My view is that either the second or the third position can be maintained and defended by a Christian. As we shall see later, one who holds the second position may be forced, if he is going to be a real Christian, to adhere to or practice the third position.

ADDITIONAL QUESTIONS

Assuming that many and doubtless most of you attend the movies at least some and that you would defend the second of the three positions suggested, there are two or three additional questions of major importance.

"How often should one attend?"

Let us repeat that one should not attend at all if he cannot do so in good conscience. If one does not consider attendance wrong within itself, he should select only the best shows. If he does that, will it not place a considerable limit on his attendance? If his standards are as high as they should be, will he not find comparatively few shows that he, in good conscience, can and should attend?

Is it not also possible that if he is as busy as he should be, he will not have time for many shows? Christians are not justified in neglecting more important matters to attend the movies. As God's stewards, we are responsible to him for the use of our time, and, incidentally, also for our money.

"What about Sunday shows?"

This question is asked frequently. Do you not believe that it would be answered for Christians, young or old, if they would apply the tests of effect (the three questions), of secrecy, of universality, and of prayer? As a part of the test of effect, let one examine his own reaction to attendance on Sunday. Does his better self approve? Does there tend to be a decreased interest in the church, the church's program, and in things spiritual?

It also might help one if he would apply the test of appropriateness to Sunday movie attendance. Sunday is observed as a holy day, because it was the day on which Christ arose from the dead. His resurrection completed God's program for our redemption. Do you think it is appropriate for a Christian on that day to attend a movie? You know what my answer is: what is yours?

"What if others disapprove one's attendance?"

This question applies only to those who do not consider it wrong for a Christian to attend selected shows. What if he discovers that it would hurt his influence for good if he attended?

If we accept the basic Christian principles, set out formerly, there can be only one answer. Regardless of what one's personal viewpoint may be, once he is convinced that participation in any activity will hurt his influence for Christ and his cause, that should settle the matter for him. Paul's principle of eating meat offered to idols applies here. There are two verses in 1 Corinthians 10 that would answer most of the questions asked by a sincere Christian concerning right and wrong. They are as follows: "Let no one seek his own good, but the good of his neighbor" (v. 24) and "So whether you eat or drink, or whatever you do, do all to the glory of God" (v. 31).

What is your personal conclusion concerning the rightness or wrongness of movie attendance? I do not mean that all of you are mature enough to be left entirely free to make your own decision. Some of you certainly should give serious consideration to the judgment of your parents and of other mature, consecrated Christians and church leaders.

Wise parents and leaders, however, want you to accept more and more of the responsibility for your own decisions. This is a phase of the maturing process. Many of you are at the age when the controls are being shifted from your parents to you. Others of you are already away from home and hence are on your own. The more your decision concerning movies, or anything else, can be a personal one, the more it will be a part of you and the deeper will be its influence in your life.

You are fortunate if you have built into your life fundamental Christian ideals and moral principles that will give you the resources to make wise decisions. If you have, you will develop stability of character. You will become increasingly well adjusted to life and its problems.

It is hoped that whatever conclusion you reach concerning this and other problems will be deliberate, thoughtful, and prayerful. You need to arrive at a position you can defend as a Christian. You should have real convictions and should be able to state your convictions clearly without appearing to be self-righteous.

In thinking through your relation to the movies, ask the questions, apply the tests, utilize the sources of light, as suggested in previous chapters. Does your practice conform to your theoretical conclusions?

12

SUNDAY OBSERVANCE

What do you ordinarily do on Sunday? List, at least in your mind, everything that went into the making of last Sunday, from the time you arose in the morning until you went to bed at night. As you think back over the things you did, do you have some question concerning the rightness or wrongness of any of the activities of the day? Do you know people who do things on Sunday of which you disapprove? If so, why do you disapprove?

BACKGROUND

In seeking to determine what is right or wrong to do on Sunday, we may derive some benefit from a brief study of the biblical background for the day we call Sunday. The word "Sunday" is not found in the Bible. We do find many references to the sabbath, which was, in a sense, the forerunner of Sunday and, in another sense, was replaced by Sunday.

When God had completed his creative work, he "blessed the seventh day and hallowed it, because on it God rested from all his work which he had done in creation" (Gen. 2:3). Later, God commanded his people to keep the seventh day holy. He considered its observance important enough to include it in the Ten Commandments. These commandments summarize the basic moral laws of the Old Testament.

We should remember that these laws are just as binding upon us today, as they were upon those to whom they were first given. We also should not forget that those laws are not the arbitrary requirements of some oriental despot. God's fundamental laws are written into our natures and into the nature of the universe in which we live. They operate for our good.

Some people suggest that we do not keep the seventh day; that our holy day is not the Old Testament sabbath but Sunday or the first day of the week. Since this is true, they imply that Christians are not obligated to observe the Old Testament laws concerning the sabbath. It is true that the Christian Sunday takes the place of the Jewish sabbath, but it is just as true that God's laws for the sabbath are applicable to our Sunday. The fundamental moral laws of the Old Testament have not been repealed or abolished. God's laws concerning the sabbath are part of them.

Also, the Old Testament sabbath and the New Testament "first day of the week" are more closely related than many people realize. God completed his creative work in six days and rested on the seventh day. He completed his re-creative work for man, his program for the redemption of man, on the first day of the week, the day on which Christ arose from the dead. The disciples, before the close of the New Testament period, were keeping this first day as their day of rest and worship.

It seems that the New Testament Christians had some difficulty deciding on a name for their holy day. Usually, they simply referred to it as "the first day of the week." The disciples at Troas "on the first day of the week, . . . were gathered together to break bread" (Acts 20:7) and to hear Paul's message. Paul admonished the Corinthian Christians as follows: "On the first day of every week, each one of you is to put something aside and store it up, as he may prosper, so that contributions need not be made when I come" (1 Cor. 16:2). The first day was evidently the regular day on which they came together to worship the Lord.

John, on the island of Patmos, gave a name to this day, a name which is still used by some people. He said, "I was in the Spirit on the Lord's day" (Rev. 1:10). It was the Lord's day, because it was the day on which the Lord arose from the dead.

PRINCIPLES

Several principles are found in the teachings of Jesus concerning the sabbath. These principles grew out of the controversy of Jesus with the Pharisees about the sabbath, which was one of the chief points of his conflict with them. An important principle to remember is the fact that Jesus respected the sabbath day. The Scripture says, "he went to the synagogue, as his custom was, on the sabbath day" (Luke 4:16). He did not have much respect, however, for some of the Jewish traditions regarding the observance of the day.

The Pharisees had made sabbath observance a burden to the people. They had gone to the extreme in interpreting what it meant to rest on the sabbath day. For example, the disciples of Jesus, in going through a grain field on the sabbath, pulled some heads of grain (barley or rye) and rubbed it out in their hands and ate it. Some of the Pharisees complained: "Why are you doing what is not lawful to do on the sabbath?" (Luke 6:2). The plucking and rubbing out of the grain, for the Pharisees, was work and hence unlawful on the sabbath.

They also objected to the healing miracles performed by Jesus on the sabbath. The principles he set out respecting the sabbath resulted, in the main, from his reaction to this opposition. He stated, for example, that "The sabbath was made for man, not man for the sabbath" (Mark 2:27). The Pharisees by their detailed regulations had reversed the divine order. They had forgotten that God who made man provided the sabbath for his good.

Another principle that Jesus set out, in his controversy with the Pharisees, was that "it is lawful to do good on the sabbath" (Matt. 12:12). He implied that the Pharisees would lift a sheep out of a pit on the sabbath. Man is of more value than a sheep. Therefore, he reasoned, it was and is lawful or right to heal on the sabbath.

Still another principle stated by Jesus was the fact that "The Son of man is lord [master—Goodspeed] of the sabbath" (Luke 6:5). He was master or lord of the sabbath in the sense that he was free to do what he wanted to do on the sabbath. He is also master or lord of the sabbath in the sense that he has the right to command concerning the sabbath.

These principles by Jesus concerning the sabbath are fully applicable to the Christian's Sunday. They will help us in a time of decision if we will apply them intelligently and consistently. For example, in applying the principle that the sabbath was made for man, let us ask ourselves: would participation in this activity on Sunday be best for me, for men in general, for my nation, for the entire social order? In considering the matter we should be sure to keep in mind the higher levels of human personality, the levels where men function most fully and distinctly as human beings, made in the image of God.

Now, let us consider the place of worship, work, and play in the proper observance of the Lord's day.

WORSHIP

A considerable portion of every Lord's day should be given by all his children to his worship and service. Christians, from the youngest to the oldest, ought to be in the teaching, training, and worship services of their church every Sunday unless providentially hindered. And "providentially" should not be interpreted too loosely.

The deepest longings of man's soul find their fulfilment or satisfaction in fellowship with God. The sabbath or Sunday as a day of worship is provided for man's good. How tragic if he neglects the main thing on the Lord's day!

True worship not only satisfies the deepest hunger of man, but it also lifts and stimulates every phase of his personality. One who has become conscious of the presence of the living God— and he has not worshipped unless he has been conscious of God's presence—will be better off physically and will be able to think more clearly and creatively.

This proper observance of the Lord's day, which means reserving a considerable part of it for worship and service, not only is good for men as individuals but also for society. True worship gives to the worshipper clearer insights into God's will for the world, as well as the inspiration or dynamic to go out into the world and seek to make the vision he has received from the Lord a reality among men.

Possibly this broader, social influence of worship is the background for the statement by Gladstone—one of England's greatest statesmen, and also one of her greatest Christians—that he went to church on Sunday because he loved England. The Frenchman, de Tocqueville, in speaking of the secret to America's greatness, said that he thought it was "chiefly because the spirit of the Pilgrim Fathers had so permeated the people that as a whole they take one day in seven to stop and reflect and worship." Our own Emerson wrote: "What greater calamity can befall a nation than loss of worship?" Sunday, with its worship, is necessary for the well-being of man, society and the institutions of society, the nation, and even civilization.

Are we using the proper portion of Sunday for worship and for the spiritual renewal that comes through worship? This question is more significant than any we can ask about the rightness or wrongness of specific work or recreational activities on Sunday.

WORK

Jesus said it was lawful to do good on the sabbath. Our difficulty is determining what "good" includes. We have no question about the work of a doctor, a nurse, or others who minister to the relief of human suffering. Jesus himself healed on the sabbath day.

There are also some tasks around the home about which we seldom, if ever, have any questions. Meals must be prepared, dishes washed, beds made; and, if we live on a farm, cows must be milked, chickens fed, and many other chores performed.

But our complex, industrialized social order creates some problems for us. It seems that the wheels of society cannot be kept moving unless many people work on Sunday. For example, a modern city would be almost paralyzed if its public utilities were not kept in full operation on Sunday. This cannot be done without some people working. There are other types of service activities that seemingly must operate on Sunday.

Admitting that some Sunday work is necessary, there are still some rather disturbing questions. One of these is: Is it not true that there is a lot of unnecessary Sunday work? What do you think? What about the operation of fruit stands and grocery stores on Sunday, a practice that is prevalent in many communities? Can you think of other examples of unnecessary Sunday work?

Another question, closely related to the main emphasis of these chapters, is: What should a Christian do about purchasing on Sunday? Do you think the Christian should restrict his purchases to the minimum? For example, it may be necessary in an emergency for him to have a prescription filled on Sunday; but what about his gas tank? Many of those who are forced to work on Sunday desire the privilege of having the day for worship and rest. Should not Christians do what they can to make this possible for them?

An additional question that doubtless some of you face is: Should I accept a job that will require me to work on Sunday? The answer to this question will have to be a personal matter. My judgment is that at least during the period of your moral and spiritual maturing, it will not be wise for you to accept a job requiring you to work on Sunday. Unquestionably, it will not be wise for you to have work that will prevent your regular participation in the teaching, training, and worship services of your church.

In choosing your life's vocation, should not some consideration be given to the demands it will make on your Sundays? This does not mean that this one thing should be the determining factor in the choice, but it does mean that it should be considered in making the decision.

PLAY

It is in the play or amusement area that many young people have their most serious questions regarding the proper use of the Lord's day. Most of you will discover that the matter of Sunday recreation will be decreasingly a problem as you mature spiritually and particularly as you get busier about the work of the Lord.

How can you, now and in the future, decide what is right or wrong for you to do on Sunday? Review and apply the questions, the tests, and the sources of light set out in earlier chapters. Also use the test of appropriateness suggested in the preceding chapter.

Might the following negative propositions be of help to a Christian in his time of decision concerning Sunday recreation?

We should do nothing on Sunday:

(1) That would unfit us for the tasks of the coming week.

(2) That would violate what our own Christian conscience tells us is right for us to do.

(3) That would hurt our influence as Christians.

(4) That would make it more difficult for our church to do its work in the community and in the world.

(5) That would be inappropriate for a child of God to do on the day on which Christ arose.

(6) That we felt, after prayer, was not approved by our Heavenly Father.

(7) That would prohibit our attendance at the regular services of our church.

A TEST

On the basis of the above and of other negative and positive principles that you may think of, why not make a simple test? Rate the following, according to your judgment, as to their rightness or wrongness as Sunday activities for Christians. Do this either by rating from 1 through 20 the appropriateness of the activities or by dividing them into three groups: (1) those unquestionably right or good, (2) those that are doubtful, and (3) those unquestionably wrong or bad.

_____ Attend carnival or fair.
_____ Attend picture show.
_____ Attend professional ball game.
_____ Attend Sunday school.
_____ Attend Training Union.
_____ Attend worship service.

_____ Carry papers.
_____ Go driving.
_____ Go fishing.
_____ Go swimming.
_____ Participate in Sunday evening fellowship.
_____ Play baseball (amateur).
_____ Play professional ball (football or baseball).
_____ Play tennis.
_____ Prepare lessons for school.
_____ Read Bible.
_____ Visit friends.
_____ Visit a park or zoo.
_____ Work in drug store.

13

SMOKING

Have you already made your decision concerning smoking? If you have not, you doubtless will before long. For some of you, this will be a lifetime commitment. Others of you will face the matter more than once during your life. Regardless of what is your practice now or what you contemplate doing about it in the future, I hope you will think through the question of smoking carefully and prayerfully.

If you would like to read a good brief booklet on the subject, secure *What About Smoking?* by C. Aubrey Hearn, published by School and College Service, Columbus, Ohio. I am using some facts and figures from his booklet, from some magazine articles, and from one or two books, but I shall not burden you with many references.

WHAT THE CIGARETTE ADVERTISEMENTS IMPLY

I assume that the main question you face concerning the use of tobacco is cigarette smoking. That is the reason our discussion is limited to cigarettes. However, what is said will apply, in the main, to the use of tobacco in any form.

The cigarette manufacturers spend an enormous amount of money for advertising in newspapers and magazines, on the radio and television. Some of the most attractive advertisements in leading magazines and some of the most appealing programs, particularly to young people, on the radio and television are sponsored by cigarette companies.

They have sought, with considerable success, to sell the idea that smoking is *the* thing to do. They imply that the really successful people, even in the field of athletics, smoke. Many distinguished Americans have permitted their names to be used to advertise a particular brand of cigarettes.

The advertising campaign of the cigarette manufacturers evidently has been quite successful. One study revealed that two out of every three men and three out of five women smoke. During the past twenty-five years the population has increased 35 per cent while cigarette consumption has increased 1500 per cent. During a recent year the American people consumed 395,000,-000,000 cigarettes and expended $4,300,000,000 for them. The per capita consumption including men, women, and children increased from 46 per person in 1903 to 2,500 fifty years later. The latter would be increased to 3,600 cigarettes per person if only those of smoking age were considered.

If one will observe cigarette advertisements carefully, he will discover that the manufacturers admit, by implication, that other brands of cigarettes are hurtful. For example, the following slogan was used by one cigarette manufacturing company in its radio program a short time ago: "Moisturized to cut down throat irritation." Notice that the company did not say "cut out" but "cut down." The implication was that there would be less throat irritation if one smoked that particular brand in preference to others.

A current magazine contains three cigarette advertisements, each of which implies, to some degree, that cigarettes are harmful. One says in the boldest type on the page, "——————— agree with *your* throat." Another advises, "For a Treat instead of a Treatment smoke ——————." A king-size or long cigarette makes the claim: "——————— filters the smoke 85 millimeters for your protection." If cigarette smoking was not injurious, do you suppose the manufacturers would imply that it is? Since the recent revelations by medical science concerning the relation of smoking to certain diseases the cigarette manufacturers have been a little more careful in their advertising.

What the Coaches Say

Athletic coaches are interested in producing winning teams, and, if they are the kind of coaches they ought to be, they are also interested in building character. Smoking does not fit in with either of these phases of their program.

In seven years of high school and college athletics, I never had a coach who approved or permitted smoking by the members of his squad or team. "No smoking" is one training rule, so far as I know, universally advocated by coaches.

Hearn cites statements from personal letters to him from such famous coaches as Frank Leahy of Notre Dame, Bennie Oosterbaan of the University of Michigan, Bud Wilkinson of the University of Oklahoma, Matty Bell of Southern Methodist University, and Blair Cherry who was at that time head football coach at the University of Texas.

Frank Leahy in a rather carefully worded statement said:

In coaching a football team, our greatest dislike for smoking by competing athletes is based upon the belief that its use weakens will power. The smoker submits to the pleasures of the senses too readily, with the net effect being that in other ventures he will not be willing to pay the price for ultimate success. Considered purely from the physical, smoking acts to retard the reflexes. The one getting the jump on his opponent in athletics is the one who usually is in a commanding position. A nonsmoker has a psychological advantage in that his confidence in his physical condition will always operate to his advantage.

Bud Wilkinson summed it up by saying, "In my opinion, smoking doesn't help anybody—high school students, college students, or adults."

My first football coach, who had played for one of the schools in the Big Ten Conference, said to the fellows on our squad: "You may be a good football player and smoke; you would be a better one if you did not smoke." He also frequently said, "I may not see you smoke, but when the going gets rough on the field, I'll know if you have been smoking." You know what he meant. It would be revealed by a lack of "wind" or stamina. No athlete can be at his best and smoke.

WHAT MEDICAL SCIENCE REVEALS

While all doctors do not agree concerning the wisdom of smoking, yet every study, so far as I know, that has been made of the effects of smoking by a reputable doctor or group of doctors, has produced evidence of its injurious effects. Check the current magazines for recent reports. Dr. Raymond Pearl, Johns Hopkins University, studied some years ago the effects of smoking on the death rate. He found for those thirty to sixty years of age that the death rate for heavy smokers was 61 per cent higher and for moderate smokers 14 per cent higher than for non-smokers. One writer, on the basis of Dr. Pearl's figures, worked out the following rather graphic computations: "The heavy smoker pays with 34.6 minutes of life for each cigarette he smokes. The pack-a-day smoker pays with 11.5 hours for each pack he smokes."

One of the most significant recent studies was by Doctors Hammond and Horn and their associates under the guidance of the American Cancer Society. It queried 187,000 men, fifty to seventy years of age, as to whether they smoked and how much. After eighteen months it was discovered that 4,854 deaths had occurred in the group. The death rate among regular smokers was one and one-half times greater than among the non-smokers. Heavy smokers died of heart disease at twice the rate of those who had never smoked. The cancer death rate was two and one-half times greater for heavy cigarette smokers than for non-smokers. The death rate for cancer of the lung was at least five times greater among the heavy smoking group.[1] A recent report by the American Cancer Society stated that the chances of death by heart attack are increased by 95 per cent by heavy cigarette smoking. The chances of dying from cancer are increased by 156 per cent. Alton Ochsner, famous physician of New Orleans and one of the pioneers in pointing out the bad effects of smoking, concludes that even light cigarette smoking is associated with an increasing death rate.[2]

There seems to be no doubt that there is a connection between the increase in cigarette smoking and the increase in cancer of the throat, mouth, stomach, and particularly in the increase of lung cancer. The more and the longer one smokes the greater the risk

[1] Charles S. Cameron, M.D., "Lung Cancer and Smoking," *The Atlantic* Vol. 197, No. 1 (January, 1956), p. 73.

[2] Alton Ochsner, *Smoking and Cancer* (New York: Julian Messner, 1954), p. 48.

he runs. The American Cancer Society has revealed that there are more Americans who are dying today of lung cancer than died of all types of cancer fifty years ago. Ochsner suggests that anyone who uses tobacco in any form is a candidate for cancer. His conclusion is that "proof has been piled upon proof associating the effects of compulsive smoking with cancer, with heart disease, with general respiratory and other diseases." [3]

It is generally agreed that most of the harm that comes from using tobacco is from tar, or a substance the tar contains, and from nicotine, one of the most deadly poisons. It is estimated that the average smoker takes into his lungs slightly less than a quart of tar each year. The benzapyrene it contains is a chemical capable of producing cancer.

Have you noticed a cigarette smoker blow smoke through a handkerchief? It left a brown stain. That stain was caused by incompletely burned tar products. It is like the soot in a chimney.

A killing dose of nicotine is only slightly more than an average smoker absorbs into his blood stream each day. One thing that saves the smoker is the fact that the nicotine which is absorbed very rapidly into the blood stream is also eliminated rapidly.

WHAT COMMON SENSE DICTATES

When you consider what the cigarette advertisements imply, what the coaches say, and what medical science reveals, what do you think common sense would dictate? Doctor Ochsner says, "I marvel how intelligent individuals calmly go about killing themselves." Doctor Cameron suggests that if a relation between cancer of the lung and the eating of spinach could be as clearly established as it has been between cancer of the lung and smoking, there would not be any question about the elimination of spinach from the national diet.[4] Does it not seem that the Christian would not need to go beyond common sense to get an adequate answer for the smoking problem?

Have you observed any bad effects of smoking in the lives of

[3] *Ibid.*, p. 5.
[4] Cameron, *op. cit.*, p. 75.

young people you know? Are some failing to achieve their best on the athletic field or in the classroom because they smoke? Do you remember that we suggested this approach as one source of light when we are faced with a decision concerning right or wrong?

What would common sense say to a habit as expensive, directly and indirectly, as smoking? One estimate is that the per capita expenditure by smokers for cigarettes is $62 per year. This may not seem to be very much, but it is a tithe of $620 and is considerably more than twice the per capita gifts of one of the largest religious bodies in the United States.

For the total cost of smoking, we would have to add the loss by fires started by careless smokers. Hearn suggests that for a recent year 30 per cent of all fires were attributed to smoking. Fires due to smoking increase the fire insurance rates in cities and must be charged with part of the expense of every fire department.

Those who investigated such disastrous fires as the Ringling Brothers and Barnum and Bailey Circus fire at Hartford, Connecticut, with the loss of 168 lives; the Hotel Winecoff fire, Atlanta, Georgia, with the loss of 119 lives; and the Texas City, Texas, disaster, with the estimated loss of 575 lives, say that all of these were probably caused by the careless flipping of a lighted cigarette.

What would common sense dictate about a habit that tends to enslave? There is no doubt about smoking being habit forming. For some and possibly for most smokers it becomes a habit that enslaves. If they have smoked very long, they find it very difficult to break the habit, and adjustment will be long and unpleasant. Will you not agree that man, particularly a Christian, was not made for such enslavement?

WHAT THE CHRISTIAN CONSCIENCE COMMANDS

What common sense dictates, surely the Christian conscience should and will command. As suggested previously, good religion is good common sense. This does not mean that the two can be equated or that what one discovers through common sense exhausts the Christian conception of life. It does mean that when properly understood, the Christian view of life is inclusive of all that common sense would dictate, but that it goes beyond and would give a spiritual base for and direction to common sense.

For example, when one knows the effects of smoking on the body, common sense would dictate that he not smoke. This would be true for non-Christians as well as Christians. The Christian, however, has a deeper, more meaningful motivation. He recognizes that his body belongs to the Lord. It is to be presented as a living sacrifice, holy, acceptable to God (Rom. 12:1). Not only does his body belong to God but he belongs to God: his mind, his total personality, his time, his money. Anything that keeps him from being and doing his best for God and for his fellow man should be left out of his life.

A successful business man who neither drinks nor smokes, although practically all of his business associates do, was asked for an explanation of the high standards he maintains. His reply was, "When the cigarettes or the drinks are passed, anyone can say yes. It takes someone with will power to say no, thank you. I prefer to be that someone."

Anyone can drift with the crowd. It takes one with purpose and backbone to become a leader of the crowd. Will you not agree that Christians should lead the crowd rather than be led by the crowd? Should they not set the moral pace, rather than have that pace set for them?

14

DRINKING

Some of you may ask, "Why should a question be raised about the rightness or wrongness of drinking? Everybody knows that it is not right or wise for one to drink beverage alcohol in any form." But does everybody know?

If the number of people in the United States who drink (65,-000,000—60 per cent of the population 15 years of age and over), the amount they drink (an average of 45 gallons per drinker and 69 gallons per family—drinkers and non-drinkers), and the money they spend for drink (about ten billion dollars a year—an average of $203.06 for every family), are any indication, then there are plenty of people in the United States who need to think through or to re-think their position concerning alcoholic beverages. The total drink bill is considerably more than is spent for all forms of education and is one and three-fourths times as much as the nation's milk bill.

I judge that some of you associate with young people who drink, and a few of you come from homes where alcoholic drinks are served at least on special social occasions. Drinking has or will become a real problem for many of you.

I also assume that many of you have committed yourselves to a life program of total abstinence. Others of you are in the process of deciding your relation to alcohol. Possibly some of you have participated in some so-called social drinking. It is my hope, whatever your present practice or position may be, that you will be led to think through to an intelligent, defensible, Christian position.

As a background for a wise decision, let us consider some of the effects of beverage alcohol.

ENDANGERS HEALTH

The fact that drinking endangers health is proved by the practice followed by insurance companies of asking applicants if they use alcohol. If the applicant is a regular user of alcohol, he is either denied insurance, or he is required to pay a higher rate for it. There are some companies that write policies only for non-drinkers, or they give a preferred rate to non-drinkers.

Beverage alcohol, in many ways, contributes to ill health and to a general lowering of physical efficiency. For example, there is abundant evidence that alcohol damages the lining of the stomach and intestines. It is acknowledged also to be a main cause of cirrhosis of the liver, a disease in which the liver shrinks and hardens. Furthermore, alcohol weakens the kidneys and is a factor, indirectly and directly, in many other diseases such as cancer, tuberculosis, heart trouble, and venereal disease.

Drinking also contributes to ill health by lowering one's resistance to disease. Alcohol does this both directly and indirectly. Its use lowers the body's resistance to disease germs, and, in addition, the drinker neglects his health while under the influence of alcohol. The life expectancy of the drinker is less than that of the non-drinker.

The Boy Scout Merit Badge pamphlet entitled *Personal Health* reveals something that may surprise you. It says that the death rate among steady, moderate drinkers, who are regarded as temperate persons, is almost twice as much as for non-users of alcohol. It is 186 as compared to 100.

The physical effects of alcohol is one reason many great athletes and coaches are opposed so strongly to all forms of beverage alcohol. Twenty-one college athletes who made "all-American" football teams in a recent year, in letters to Allied Youth, said they did not drink.[1] In the list were such well-known names as "Choo-choo" Justice of the University of North Carolina, Doak

[1] Allied Youth is an organization that makes the educational approach to the alcohol problem and organizes Allied Youth Posts in high schools. Its headquarters are at 1709 M Street, N. W., Washington 6, D. C.

Walker of Southern Methodist, Leon Hart of Notre Dame, Dick Harris of Texas, Eddie Price of Tulane, Tommie Thompson of William and Mary, Normal Meseroll of Tennessee, and Clyde Scott of Arkansas.

Let a couple of outstanding football players give their personal testimonies. Bob Williams, great quarterback of Notre Dame, said: "I've never taken a drink in my life and don't plan on starting now. From what I've seen, it seems that people think it is smart to drink, but this is a false concept. No one has ever been known to go wrong by refusing a drink." Similarly, Billy Vessels, Oklahoma backfield star, who in 1952 received the Heisman trophy as the outstanding college football player in the nation, stated: "I am a total abstainer from alcoholic beverages since I am convinced that drinking is not synonymous with success or popularity on the football field or in life. I think it is smarter not to drink and that maximum abilities are not realized by the boy or girl who lacks the courage to say, 'No, thank you.'"

Do we need to go any further in a search for an answer to the question "Is it right or wrong to drink?" Is not the case against drinking strengthened, however, when we remember that the Christian's body belongs to God, that it is the dwelling place of the Holy Spirit?

IMPAIRS MIND AND PERSONALITY

One of the leading American students of the effects of beverage alcohol declares as follows: "The chief effect of alcohol in whatever doses or concentration it may be injected is upon the functions of the brain—those functions which express the will, the emotions, memory, attention, reason, intelligence, and judgment, as well as those which control muscular and sensory functions and the coordination of one with the other." [2]

C. Aubrey Hearn, in his splendid book entitled *Alcohol the Destroyer*, says, "Alcohol is universally acknowledged to be an

[2] Haven Emerson, *Alcohol: Its Effects on Man* (New York: D. Appleton-Century Co., 1934), p. 31.

enemy of the mind. It has been called the 'befuddling beverage.' " [3] It has, as he suggests, an affinity for the brain.

The fact that alcohol makes its first and most immediate attack on the brain is particularly significant. It tends to paralyze, at least temporarily, the very functions that set man apart from the animal creation. In other words, alcohol tends to pull man down to the animal level. One of its most noticeable effects is the removal of inhibitions. Under the influence of alcohol, one will say and do things that otherwise he would never say or do.

Alcohol causes one to lose, to a considerable degree, his power to distinguish between the wise and the foolish, the proper and the improper, the right and the wrong. The prophet Isaiah long ago spoke of priests and prophets who "reel with strong drink, they are confused with wine, they stagger with strong drink; they err in vision, they stumble in giving judgment" (Isa. 28:7).

This erring in vision and the confusing effects of alcohol are the things that make the drinking driver such a menace on the highway. In a recent year the death toll from motor vehicle accidents in the United States was 35,000, with an additional 1,225,-000 injured. In one-fourth of the fatal accidents, according to the National Safety Council, either the driver or the pedestrian was reported to have been drinking.

One report suggests that alcohol contributes to accidents because it results in blurred or double vision, narrowed or tunnel vision, shortens the range of sight, makes one blind to color, impairs judgment, and delays hand reaction and, even more, foot reaction.[4] Alcohol is just as definitely a menace in the shop or factory as it is on the highway.

ENSLAVES THE INDIVIDUAL

One of the most serious charges against beverage alcohol is that it tends to make slaves of those who drink it. The first drink

[3] Nashville: Convention Press, 1956, p. 58. Hearn has written a more recent book, *The Way to Sobriety* (Cincinnati: The Standard Publishing Foundation, 1955).

[4] W. Russell Shull (ed.), *The Alcohol Problem Visualized* (5th ed.; Chicago: National Forum, Inc., 1950), pp. 29–37.

frequently leads to another and to increasingly more frequent drinks. A drink of small alcoholic content tends to lead to one that is stronger. The law of habit works, and the individual, before he may be aware of it, has become a slave to alcohol.

This does not mean that everyone who takes a drink will end up a drunkard. Statistics reveal, however, that there are approximately 4,500,000 alcoholics in the United States, with several million more excessive or problem drinkers.

Young people who are considering drinking should remember that alcohol is a notorious liar. As the Scripture verse says, "Wine is a mocker, strong drink a brawler; and whoever is led astray by it is not wise" (Prov. 20:1). It might be well for us to remember what Dr. Ralph Overman, chairman of the Special Training Division of the Oak Ridge Institute of Nuclear Studies, once said to a group of boys and girls: "When you have drunk one drink, you are one drink drunk." This is true whether that one drink was beer, wine, or whiskey.

Some people have more of a weakness for alcohol than others, but "No one can tell who can indulge without overindulging." Dr. E. M. Jellinek, generally considered America's leading authority on alcohol, suggests: "Science has found no way to determine or distinguish who or what sort of a drinker may or may not become an alcoholic." Is it not just plain common sense for one to abstain entirely from all forms of beverage alcohol? "At the last it bites like a serpent, and stings like an adder."

CORRUPTS SOCIETY

In determining what is right or wrong for one to do, a Christian must not only consider the influence of the particular activity upon him but also its influence on others and on the social order. One of the chief counts against beverage alcohol is its effect on society. It corrupts everything it touches.

The home more than any other social institution is directly affected by alcohol which contributes to the instability of many homes and is a factor in many divorces. District judges of a Southern city recently said it was the most frequent cause for divorce.

Innocent children are its chief victims. Aubrey Hearn quotes Edwin Lewis as follows: "If you ask, why should I abstain from alcoholic drink? let this be an answer: For the sake of little children." Theodore F. Adams is also quoted as follows: "The home has no greater enemy than liquor in all its forms. . . . There is only one safe way to handle it. Leave it alone."

Alcohol also directly corrupts the state, which is another basic social institution. It creates many problems for the state. It is closely related to many forms of crime. The liquor industry itself has always tended to be lawless, even when it is legal. The state pays dearly for the taxes from the liquor business.

WHAT DO YOU THINK?

What are the most commonly expressed justifications for drinking? If you made a list of those you have heard young people give, would your list include the following? "Because others are doing it." "It is expected by the crowd with which I run." "It is expected by the boys [or girls] I date." "It would be rude to refuse." "It is something to do." "It helps one to have a good time." "One needs to know how to drink moderately." "It enables one to forget some things for a while." "My parents drink." "Many prominent people I know drink."

Examine these and other reasons frequently given for drinking. Will they stand the test of intelligent analysis? Is it not true that several of them reveal the attitude of a child rather than a mature person? One who is mature is supposed to be able to make up his own mind and stand on his own feet. If one wants to be a man or a woman who will lead others, he cannot drift with them and let them determine what he will do.

When one mentions the men of distinction who drink, would it not be the smart thing to remember that there are many more "men of extinction" who drink, and some of them were once men of distinction?

A doctor's judgment is as follows: "Definitely, competent medical workers feel that no one under twenty-one should *experiment at all* with drinking any alcoholic beverages, including beer . . .

medical science has concluded *that it's much smarter for anyone —under or over twenty-one—not to drink.*" [5]

POSTSCRIPT: THE DRUG MENACE

This problem is one of serious proportions, yet it was not considered of sufficient concern to enough Christian youth to justify a separate chapter. Since beverage alcohol is a narcotic, this brief postscript should be added to this chapter.

Although the prevalence of the use of drugs and drug addiction among teen-agers has been exaggerated by some people, nevertheless there has been enough of an increase to justify the deepening concern about the problem. One writer, in a rather careful and conservative study of the matter, concludes: "The incidence of drug addiction among adolescents has undoubtedly multiplied many times in the past few years, and confronts us today with a special problem of potentially grave proportions." [6]

The most widely used drug among teen-agers is marihuana. Its use has spread rapidly in recent years. Its immediate effects are bad enough, but in addition many marihuana users "graduate" to heroin, to get a bigger "kick." The latter is the most frequently used opiate among American addicts.

Before closing this postscript, possibly a statement should be made concerning the use of sleeping pills. Deutsch says their use has become a major drug menace. All of us need to remember that one can become enslaved to barbiturates just as he can to other narcotics. The use of such pills, except as prescribed by a doctor, is unwise and dangerous. Also, their use may be a sign of character weakness. It may be an evidence of the prevalent tendency to escape the burdens, the pains, and the unpleasant responsibilities of life. We should guard against dependence upon the simplest pain relievers. Why not be mature enough to face life courageously and all that it brings?

[5] Robert V. Seliger, *It's Smarter Not to Drink* (Columbus, Ohio: School and College Service, 1949), p. 7. A booklet of 32 pages.

[6] Albert Deutsch, *What We Can Do About the Drug Menace* (New York: Public Affairs Committee, 1952). This is Public Affairs Pamphlet, No. 186.

15

DANCING

"What is wrong with dancing?" The question came from an attractive, popular college sophomore across the table from me. She said she had danced for years and did not see any harm in it. She had heard the matter discussed by Christian leaders, but they had not been very convincing.

By repeating this question I do not mean to prejudge dancing. It is the usual way the dancing problem is introduced in a personal conference or in a group discussion. I am going to assume, as I did with that college sophomore, that you honestly want to know if there is anything wrong with dancing. I wish we could discuss the matter personally or in a group where I could have the advantage of your questions and comments.

Now, what about dancing? How does it fit into the general picture for the Christian?

DEFENSE OF DANCING

There are many young people and older people who dance and defend their participation by one or more of the following arguments.

Some suggest, "Dancing gives one grace and poise." We cannot take the space to examine each of these arguments or reasons in detail, but does dancing give one physical poise and grace of bearing?

"It is enjoyable," is another defense. We cannot question the truthfulness of the statement. Many dance because they like the music, thrill to the rhythmic movement over the floor, enjoy being in the crowd, and get an emotional lift from the whole experience. Admitting that all of this is true, would that make it right or wrong for a Christian? Should there not be a higher or a deeper basis for one's decision?

The question "Is it any worse for one person to dance than for another to pet?" was directed to a panel during a religious focus week on a college campus. What would your answer have been to the question? If the answer would have been no, would that make dancing right? Does one arrive at the right merely by a process of comparison? Carried to its ridiculous conclusion, such a method would mean that everything one did would be right except the worst thing he could do.

Still another reason frequently given for dancing is, "It expresses a natural urge." Man, by nature, has a rhythmic instinct. Would this necessarily mean that every method used to express that urge is right or wise? Is there not a difference between saying that there is nothing wrong with the innate urges of man and saying that this fact justifies or makes right every channel used to express those desires? We do not argue in that way in regard to hunger, thirst, or sex; why should we in regard to the rhythmic urge or instinct? The preceding does not mean that dancing is necessarily right or wrong; it does ask if this argument is a justifiable defense of dancing.

One of the most frequent defenses given for dancing, particularly by young people, is: "Everybody else is doing it." Sometimes "everybody," from the viewpoint of the young person, embraces prominent adult leaders in the community, including school teachers and even some church leaders, but more frequently he is referring to those of his own age group.

There are some communities where the statement "everybody dances" is almost literally true. A prominent church leader recently said: "It seems that dancing is a lost cause in our community. We can do nothing about it." However, there are some communities where most of the finest and best young people do not dance. What about your community? Is it possible that the statement "everybody is doing it" may be an excuse rather than a reason for dancing?

What if everybody did dance; would that make it right? Where is a Christian supposed to get his moral standards: from the crowd or from an inner conviction of what he considers God's will for his life? On what level should the Christian live: the instinctive, the customary, the conscience, or the Christian level?

DANCING IN THE BIBLE

The fact that "they danced in the Bible" is given by some as a defense of modern dancing. Let us look at dancing in the Bible and see if it would justify dancing by a Christian.

There are a number of references to dancing in the Bible. An examination, however, of those passages and of the words translated "dance" will reveal that dancing in the Bible had little in common with modern social dancing.

The dance in biblical times was primarily a method of expressing one's emotions. Joy filled the individual, and he expressed his joy by jumping around or whirling about. This was the type of dance participated in by David before the ark of the covenant (2 Sam. 6:14, 16).

Also, dancing, as found in the Bible, was largely spontaneous. The music and the movement were evidently in many cases improvised as the dance proceeded (see Judges 11:34 and 1 Sam. 18:6–7).

There was some organized group dancing accompanied by music and singing. The singing, at times, was responsive or antiphonal (Ex. 15:20; 1 Sam. 18:6–7). These dances may have been somewhat like our modern folk dances or rhythmic games but possibly more like some Indian dances.

Dancing in the Bible differed from modern social dancing in at least three ways: (1) movement; (2) participants; and (3) occasions or reasons for it.

There was no smooth movement of the feet over the floor as in the modern dance. The participants were usually women. "The men won the victories; the women celebrated." There is no record of men and women, boys and girls dancing together. Also, there was probably no such thing as dancing just for the sake of the dance. It was always the channel for the expression of joy for a victory or for some special occasion or blessing.

COUNTS AGAINST DANCING

Just as there are many reasons given in defense of dancing, in like manner there are many arguments against it. Let us consider some of them.

The logical place to begin is with the effect on the individual participant. Some contend that the grace and poise that dancing may give is more than counterbalanced by its harmful physical effects on those who dance. It is suggested that most people who attend a dance are not in the best condition for school or work the following day.

The late hours, with long hours of dancing, attended by considerable emotional disturbance, at least for some, leave them somewhat exhausted, although they may feel exhilarated while dancing. The danger from emotional disturbances is most serious for immature adolescent young people and seems to be particularly grave for highly sensitive teen-age girls.

Another count against dancing is that it is attended so often by many temptations. In the study, mentioned previously, which was made with the help of student secretaries on forty college campuses, it was found that the more prevalent dancing was on the campus the more prevalent were petting, drinking among both men and women students, and pre-marital sex relations and even homosexuality. This does not mean necessarily a cause and effect relation. It does mean that these problems tend to go together. Jesus taught us to pray, "And lead us not into temptation. But deliver us from evil" (Matt. 6:13).

A dean of women on a state university campus reduced noticeably the amount of drinking on the campus by restricting the number of dances the sororities could sponsor.

Possibly as strong as any argument against dancing is the fact that there are certain natural urges or passions that tend to be aroused or stirred by the bodily contact of the boy and girl in the dance. These are urges that are all right within themselves and may be used for high and holy purposes, but they should not find full expression before or outside of marriage.

The arousing of sexual passion is more frequently a problem for the boy. There are very few boys who will not admit that they are aroused by dancing with a girl. On the other hand, many girls do not know that most boys and men are more easily stimulated along this line than are women and are less easily satisfied. Dancing frequently leads to serious temptations along sex lines. A plain statement of the preceding had never been made to the sophomore college student who asked, "What is wrong with dancing?" When she saw it, and she readily did, it settled the matter for her.

One who is serious about living the Christian life, and that has been my assumption concerning you throughout these discussions, will give careful consideration to the effects of dancing or any other activity on his spiritual life. The Christian life is basically a matter of one's relation to a living, divine Person. Do you think dancing will affect the Christian's relation to God? Does it tend to affect his spiritual growth? Does it reduce his awareness of the leadership of the Spirit of God in his life? Does it influence his relation to his church?

Some Christian workers say that one of the first effects on the lives of most young people when they begin to dance is a loss of interest in the church and in things spiritual. Have you observed this effect in the lives of Christian young people you know? If it is true, does it represent a major count against dancing by a Christian?

We have frequently suggested in these chapters that a Christian should consider seriously the effects of his behavior on others. Many Christians believe that dancing will hurt one's influence with non-Christians and with Christians. What do you think? What young Christians of your acquaintance are most highly respected by non-Christian and Christian young people? Do they dance?

Some Christians who do not see a great deal of harm in dancing itself, suggest that it is unwise because it represents a movement

toward or a compromise with the world. They suggest that dancing, for some, is like the proverbial salesman's foot in the door.
Once the door is opened, it is difficult to know when, where, and
how to stop the flood tide of worldliness that tends to sweep
in.

For many churches, campuses, and individual Christians, dancing has become a pivotal, if not *the* pivotal problem. There
seems to be a tendency to let down at this point. The study referred to previously revealed that dancing was considerably more
common on college campuses than any other problem studied.

Your Answer

Possibly so far in your life, in determining what is right and
wrong, you have accepted, in the main, the judgment of your
parents or adult Christian leaders in whom you have confidence.
As recommended previously, you should continue to respect their
judgment and give serious consideration to it, yet you will never
be on solid ground, in regard to dancing or any other problem,
until you think through these matters for yourself and come to a
personal conviction concerning your relation to them. This does
not mean necessarily that you will either change your position
or have a closed mind. It does mean that you will be able to defend your position. Your moral conduct will be on a stable
foundation or basis.

Possibly you have heard someone ask, "Cannot one dance and
be a Christian?" What would be your answer? Doubtless you
would answer yes, because you know of Christians who dance.
But what would be your answer to the question: "Can one dance
and be a good Christian?" What if the question is raised to the
superlative: "Can one dance and be the best Christian?" What is
your answer to that question?

In making your decision concerning dancing, if you have not
made it already, remember the tests—the test of secrecy, the test
of universality, the test of prayer. Make those tests for yourself.
What about the highest test—prayer? Could you ask God to go
with you if you went to a dance? Could you ask him to bless you

as you dance? Could you pray for the one with whom you were dancing?

Another test, suggested previously in these discussions, is the test of personal reaction. Would there be complete inner approval if you danced? Or, would something within disapprove? Would dancing cause you to lose a little respect for yourself as a Christian? Would there be regrets the next morning?

Let us return for a moment to the idea of being a maximum Christian. Should we be satisfied to give God anything less than our best? Ought we not have a holy ambition, to use an athletic term, to play on God's first team? If we play on God's first team, must we not give up anything that will handicap us in playing the Christian game of life? When we remember what Christ has done for us, should we not give up joyously whatever we are persuaded will keep us from counting for the maximum for him? How glorious it is to remind ourselves that he never asks us to give up anything that is best for us.

If you did exactly what you think God would have you to do, what would you do about dancing? Can you give defensible reasons for your answer? If you consider dancing wrong, why do you? Is it because of the environment in which it is usually found, the attitude of people toward it, or do you consider it wrong within itself?

SQUARE DANCING

There are some communities where square dancing is much more prevalent than so-called social or ballroom dancing. What about a Christian participating in square dances? A thorough discussion would require much more space than we can give. To save space, let us assume that there is nothing wrong as such with square dancing. But we have discovered previously that this does not settle the matter for a Christian. What about the effect on the participant and particularly upon his influence for good in the community? Will square dancing pass the tests? What about the test of universality?

Let us assume again that you disapprove social dancing but do not see any harm in square dancing. Will it be easier to move from square dancing into social dancing than from no dancing of any kind to social dancing? In other words, does square dancing tend to reduce one's resistance to the word "dance" and hence to make it easier for him to participate in social dancing?

What about square dancing: is it wise or unwise for a Christian? Without attempting to follow through to a conclusion, I believe you can see my line of reasoning concerning it.

16

PETTING

Faculty members and students agreed that "heavy court-ing" was the biggest problem on their campus. By "courting" they meant what is usually called "petting." I had not been there long until I understood why they considered it the most serious prob-lem on the campus.

There are several definitions of petting but the following by Elliott and Bone is as clear as any: "Petting refers rather indis-criminately to embracing, kissing, fondling and all types of physi-cal intimacy between the sexes, whether mild or intense, and whether an expression of sincere affection or merely an emotional debauch with little or no respect for the other person involved." [1]

DEFENSE OF PETTING

There are many reasons or arguments given for petting. These may be grouped into four or five major categories.

There is the argument that petting is simply "doing what comes naturally." The implication is that doing what comes nat-urally is right, or at least that the individual should not be blamed for expressing a natural urge.

As we have said previously, no inborn desire is wrong within itself. On the other hand, a natural urge may be expressed in wrong ways or in ways that will debase man. It may be expressed in such a manner as to be self-defeating, in the sense that the hunger itself will not find the satisfaction it seeks.

Some of the urges that may find expression through petting may be natural. It is, however, the hungers or urges behind the petting that are natural, and petting itself becomes natural only

[1] *The Sex Life of Youth* (New York: Association Press, 1929), p. 62.

when it is a normal, healthy outlet for the drives that find expression through it. For example, it is natural to want to be loved
and to want someone to love. This does not mean, however, that
it is wise or right to give expression to these desires at any time,
with anyone, and in any way one desires. Such would be just as
foolish and unwise as to permit the baby to eat anything he
wants. Surely all will admit that petting is not always an expression of genuine love.

It is somewhat surprising how often the same arguments or defenses are given for a number of the activities we are considering.
Have you heard the following given to justify petting: "Everybody does it." "You have to pet to be popular." "You can't have
dates unless you pet." "It is expected." Have you ever heard a
girl say that the boy expects her to pet with him to pay for the
evening's entertainment? Do some of the boys you know claim
that the girls expect the boys to pet?

How common are the preceding attitudes among the young
people whom you know? How much justification for their attitudes? There are some communities where very popular young
people, who are sought after for dates, do not pet. Is yours such
a community?

Let us repeat some questions previously asked: "What if everybody does?" "What if it is expected?" "What if one does get
labeled?" "After all, where is a Christian supposed to get his
moral standards—from what others do, from what they expect
him to do, or from within his own soul as he prayerfully seeks to
know God's will for his life?"

There are a few young people who rather weakly and distress-
ingly complain, "If we do not pet, what can we do on a date?"
Is this primarily a defense of petting or is it a plea of helpless-
ness, an acknowledgment of intellectual and spiritual poverty?
Do you know young people who seem to lack the ability, the will,
or the initiative to plan varied and wholesome activities for their
dates? Are there not many things other than petting that young
people can do on a date that will be more abidingly satisfying to
them?

There is one defense of petting sometimes given that is very unhealthy and which reveals an unwholesome type of thinking. It is more frequently given by older young people who are involved in rather heavy petting, and who are searching for some basis on which they can justify their behavior. These young people argue that petting is a necessary part of the maturing process. It is an essential phase, so they claim, of one's preparation for marriage. They even suggest that a couple cannot know if they are suited for each other unless there are physical expressions of their love for one another. In evaluating this argument remember that the same line of reasoning is followed in defense of premarital sex relations.

There is no evidence that petting by young people is necessary or even wise preparation for marriage. It is the general opinion of students of the family that petting considerably reduces the chances that one will make the most satisfactory adjustment after marriage.

DANGERS OF PETTING

All of the following things will not inevitably result from petting but they do represent some of the major dangers of petting.

Petting tends to magnify unduly the physical in a couple's relation with one another. A love that lasts is a love that is primarily spiritual rather than physical. Love is on an unsound foundation if it is based too largely on the physical expressions of it. This is true both before and after marriage. There are legitimate, natural, and necessary physical expressions of love; but to be on the soundest basis the physical must be kept subservient to the spiritual; every physical expression must be the normal result of a genuine and pure love.

Petting also tends to disturb the emotions, particularly of immature young people. Some consider this the chief danger in petting. It seems to be particularly damaging to the girl. This does not mean that she is more aroused by the experience. The experience is more likely to be hurtful to her because she is more highly keyed nervously and emotionally than the boy. One doctor, who had many teen-age girls come to him who had become nervous and irritable and with some of their bodily functions considerably disturbed, said the condition of many of these girls was the result, to a large degree, of too much petting with its attendant nervous tension.

One source of this nervous tension, at least for some Christian young people, is inner self-condemnation. There is created within them a conflict between the ideals they have for their lives and the level on which they are living. Another source of tension for many young people is the fact that petting arouses urges that should not and cannot find proper and healthy expression outside of marriage. Any urge or emotion that cannot find some outlet creates tension.

A conference with a young woman who had a rather serious personality problem revealed that one source of her problem was the fact that, during high school and undergraduate college days, she had petted heavily. She said that she did not enjoy it, really wanted to quit, but continued simply because it seemed to be expected. She suggested that what was true of her was also true of most of the girls she knew. How general do you suppose this is?

Many young people who pet, such as the young woman just mentioned, tend to lose respect for themselves and for the ones with whom they pet. They have an inner sense of shame and guilt, but they find themselves so enmeshed in the practice that it is extremely difficult for them to free themselves. They discover that petting, like smoking, drinking, and narcotics, is habit forming. It tends to enslave and to create a desire for more.

In appraising petting, one should never forget that it leads to serious temptations and may, almost before one knows it, involve him in serious sin. Anyone who pets should know that he is playing with fire, and fire has a habit, at times, of getting out of control. The consequences may be disastrous to both the boy and the girl but particularly to the girl. A Christian young man in deep remorse said, "If anyone had told us five minutes before that we would have gone that far, I would have said, 'You don't know what you are talking about.'" Are you acquainted with any who have had to pay dearly for petting that carried them further than they ever dreamed they would go? This is not said to scare you but to help you to be realistic in your approach to the problem of petting.

One of the main charges against petting is that it cultivates a low order of love. Love should be holy and sacred. Nothing can do more than a pure love to lift and enrich life. Do you know of young people—boys or girls—whose lives have been largely made over because of a high and holy love for a fine Christian young man or woman? On the other hand, there is no one thing that can be more degrading and debasing than so-called love on a low level. The low order of love cultivated by petting tends to unfit one for the rich experiences that could be his through genuine love. A doctor expresses this idea as follows: "Petting means the cultivation of low tastes and ideas in love. He whose musical tastes have been fed on jazz is not likely to rise to the full appreciation or rendering of a masterful symphony."

Real or genuine love partakes of the divine quality. It seeks to give itself to the object loved rather than using that object for selfish personal gratification. This idea of self-giving love is a distinct contribution of Christianity to the concept of love. It is expressed by the Greek word *agape*. It is found in such expressions as: "God is love" (1 John 4:8, 16), "For God so loved the world that he gave . . ." (John 3:16), "Christ loved the church and gave himself up for her" (Eph. 5:25), and "Greater love has no man than this, that a man lay down his life for his friends" (John 15:13).

If love is to live and is to enrich one's life, it must partake of this divine quality. Does petting fit in with such a conception of love?

Many a young person sells his birthright of love at its highest and best in his home-of-the-future for a little of what he considers pleasure, but which is at best only for a brief season. In this area, as elsewhere, the best things of life are reserved for those who have the strength of character and the courage to sacrifice the lower. There is no law of life more basic than that expressed by Jesus when he said, "For whoever loses his life for my sake will find it" (Matt. 16:25).

THE DECISION CONCERNING PETTING

What should be the Christian young person's decision? If you have any question concerning petting, let me suggest again that you ask the questions, make the tests, and utilize the sources of light. If you will do those things sincerely, you can make your own decision.

It is possible that a special word should be directed to boys and men. Too frequently they feel that they are free to go as far as a girl will let them go. Will you not agree, however, that the boy has just as much responsibility as the girl to maintain the highest standards in his relations with the opposite sex?

It will help one reach a wise decision concerning petting if he will remember that man, made in the image of God, is of infinite value. This in turn means that an individual should never be treated as a means but always as an end. In other words, it is contrary to the dignity of man, created in the image of God, for him (man or woman) to be used by another as an instrument of selfish gratification. Such action debases man, God's highest creation.

We should also recall that we are our brother's keeper. We are responsible to God for what we do to and with those who, like us, are creations of God. This means that we should think of the other's welfare rather than our personal satisfaction. Can you see the relation of the preceding to petting?

Does not the Golden Rule also apply to the matter of petting? If one would like to have as a companion someone who has kept himself or herself for "the one and only," would not the application of the Golden Rule demand that he do the same? Would we prefer that others refrain from petting with our brothers and sisters? Should we not do unto the brothers and sisters of others what we would like for them to do unto our own? Is anything less than a consistent application of the Golden Rule fair?

Let us say again that we cannot discover fulness of life except as we sacrifice self or as we exercise proper self-control. We are constantly tempted to sacrifice the higher for the lower. Common sense would dictate that we sacrifice the lower for the higher.

Love, at its richest and most ennobling, can be known only by those who sacrifice or forego "a low order of love." There are few things that will give one more satisfaction than for him (or her) to be able to say, whether he actually says it or not, when the wedding day arrives, "I have kept myself absolutely for you." A joy just as great can come if the young father or mother can look their first-born squarely in the eye and say, "I kept myself clean for you." This may never be said verbally, but how glorious for the young parents to have so lived that they could say it! I hope and pray that this may be true of you. Whether it will be or not depends on you. You may be in the process now of making the decision that will determine whether or not this will be your experience.

17

POPULARITY

The craze for popularity is the biggest problem I have with my young people." This statement by a successful young pastor, who is devoted to his young people, is one reason this chapter on popularity is included in this series.

Popularity as such, of course, does not involve the problem of right or wrong. It is not necessarily right or wrong for you or any other young person to be popular. Right and wrong may enter into the picture, however, when we examine the methods one uses in an attempt to gain popularity, the place he gives to popularity in his life, or what he does with whatever popularity he may have.

WITH OR WITHOUT COMPROMISE?

Whether popularity is gained by means of or without compromise is one important factor in determining the rightness or wrongness of one's popularity. There are some campuses, some communities, and certainly some groups where one can be popular without compromising basic principles or personal convictions. There are other places or groups where popularity would necessitate compromise by a Christian.

Any popularity that is gained through compromise of moral principles and spiritual ideals is purchased at too high a price. Such popularity ultimately is self-defeating. One cannot surrender his moral integrity without damaging, sooner or later, his total personality. For the Christian such compromise will result in inner condemnation by his own better self.

It should be remembered, however, that we are discussing the compromise of basic moral principles. If we are to get along with other people, we must not be contentious concerning unimportant or non-essential matters. Some Christians become offensive to their friends as well as to their enemies because they fail to discriminate between the essential and the nonessential. They are equally dogged or tenacious in holding on to and defending the less important and the more important. This is one way "to lose friends and to fail to influence people."

It is possible for us to be uncompromising Christians and yet be agreeable, even with those with whom we may sharply differ. Most of us lose friends not so much because of what we stand for as the spirit and method with which we defend our position. The spirit of self-righteousness seems to be a rather distinctive temptation of Christians.

With Whom?

The rightness or wrongness of popularity may be determined, to some degree, by the ones with whom we are popular or desire to be popular. Usually, if one is popular with one group, he will be unpopular, to some extent, with other groups.

In other words, rather serious questions might properly be raised concerning a Christian young person if he had become generally popular on the high school or college campus but, at the same time, he had lost the respect of the best Christian young people on the campus. It would appear that he had paid a price for his popularity, a price that no Christian should pay. Thus we can see that it is possible, in some situations, for it to be a serious reflection on a Christian if he is too popular.

There can be no doubt that popularity should not be the chief thing sought by a Christian. Too strong a desire for popularity frequently will lead to compromise with the things of the world. Such a compromise will prevent us from doing what we ought to do for the Lord and for others. Those who have accomplished worth-while things for the Lord and for the world often have had to stand against the crowd; they have had to do some things that many others have not approved. Surprisingly, they have encountered, at times, opposition from within the Christian group itself.

Life's supreme search should not be for popularity but for the will of God or the kingdom of God among men. For the Christian the kingdom is the treasure hid in a field; it is the pearl of great price.

WHAT FOR?

The rightness or wrongness of popularity for the Christian depends, to a considerable degree, upon the purposes for which he desires it and will use it. The Christian should not seek popularity for its own sake. It is doubtful if he should seek it at all. Whatever popularity may come to him should come as a natural result of the kind of life he lives.

Certainly, he should not want to be popular merely to satisfy his ego. The only kind of popularity he can justifiably desire will be a popularity that will increase his opportunities for service for God and for his fellow man.

What a Christian does with whatever popularity he has will determine largely whether it will be a curse or a blessing to him and to others. A Christian should use whatever influence he has for Christian purposes. He should seek to carry the spirit of Christ into every group he touches.

A Christian student was a star football player. He found that his athletic success increased his influence on the campus. He was so uncompromisingly and wholesomely Christian on the athletic field, in the classroom, and on the campus in general, that the entire campus was lifted to higher levels of Christian living during his stay as a student. His influence lingered years after he had left the campus. He was a good steward of his influence, of the popularity he had.

All the popularity that any Christian, young or old, should have is the popularity that he will dedicate to God and to the fulfilment of God's will among men. What are we doing with what we have?

TODAY OR TOMORROW?

The value one should place on popularity also may be decided by how abiding it will be. Popularity for anyone—Christian or non-Christian—may be very uncertain and passing. One may be a hero today and a bum tomorrow. Any athlete can testify to the truthfulness of this statement.

Even the popularity of Jesus rose and fell. Doubtless many of the same people who welcomed him into Jerusalem with cries of "Hosanna!" were in the crowd, a few days later, that cried "Crucify him! Crucify him!"

The standing of Jesus in the world did not depend upon the attitude of the people toward him during the triumphal entry or during his arrest, trial, and crucifixion. He has stood through the centuries as the central, dominant personality of all history. He has been hated by some, devotedly loved by others, and respected by all who have had even a passing acquaintance with him. His influence or popularity has been abiding. One reason for this fact is that he stood for things that abide. To him the Father's will was the most important thing in life. It was to be done regardless of what people might think or do.

Much of the constructive, creative work of the world has been done by men and women who dared to do what they considered to be right, even if opposed by others. Our main question should not be "Will this be the popular thing to do" but "Is this the right thing to do?" If it is right, then we can be sure that time and the Lord are on our side. We can await the vindication that God's tomorrow will bring.

POPULARITY OR RESPECT?

"She is the most popular girl on the campus" or "He is the most popular fellow in the gang" are expressions frequently heard. What would these expressions mean on your campus or in your crowd? How is popularity measured? Is the most popular individual the one who is a member of the largest number of clubs and most frequently elected to offices on the campus? Or, is one's popularity measured in more general terms? Is the popular person on your campus or in your community one who is generally well liked by others?

If popularity is measured in the latter way, it approaches

rather closely to respect. How close it comes to genuine respect depends upon the basis for the so-called popularity. The popular individual may simply be a hail-fellow-well-met who is friendly with everyone and hence everyone is friendly with him. This is a fine quality, but abiding respect is based on something deeper. It grows out of a conviction that the individual is genuine and dependable and that he has qualities of inner worth and dignity.

There is, to a degree, a sense of reverence mixed with this type of respect. There is a feeling that the individual possesses real character. Such respect derives primarily from what the individual is rather than what he does or how he looks. It is the respected individual who is the one sought when a real friend is needed.

The Christian can properly desire to be respected by others, even by those who may not agree with all he does or refuses to do. He should seek to win the respect of people because of the consistent, effective life he lives for Christ. It should be his desire that when they need a real friend, they will turn to him for help.

We should remember, however, that our opportunities to help and to influence others will be limited if we are not friendly with all kinds of people. The Christian cannot live effectively for Christ if he separates himself from others, living his life in isolation. This is particularly true if this isolation involves a feeling of self-righteousness, a holier-than-thou attitude.

There is a need for more Christian young people who will be uncompromisingly Christian, but at the same time they will be friendly with all kinds of young people—Christian and non-Christian, good, bad, indifferent.

It is true that the dynamic Christian life must have its periods of withdrawal from others for meditation, inner renewal, and deepened insight; but such withdrawals are preparatory to more devoted and unselfish service. Following the Mount of Transfiguration comes the valley of service. Christian young people, if they are to count for Christ, must maintain a proper balance between periods of tarrying before the Lord for vision and inspiration and periods of fellowship with and service to their fellow men.

POPULAR OR UNPOPULAR?

"I do not care what anybody thinks." You have heard young people make such a statement. Do they really mean it? What has led them to say such a thing?

If we are normal, we do care what others think. One of the deepest desires of the human heart is to be approved, particularly by those we love and respect. There may be a certain stage in our development when, on the surface, we do not seem to care what adults think about what we do. Down deep, however, we do care; and even if we did not, there is at least one group whose approval we desire very much. That group is our own age group or our gang. Sometimes, we care so much about the latter that we practically become a slave to the group or gang, while at the same time we vehemently proclaim our freedom from all external control.

One who says he does not care what others think about him frequently has an inner conflict. He may want to do a certain thing that he knows will be disapproved by parents or friends. To justify his conduct he argues with himself "I do not care what they think." Or, he may have a deep desire for popularity which he has failed to achieve. He rationalizes his failure by saying "I don't care."

The latter young person may develop a martyr complex. He may seek to explain his lack of popularity by saying that one cannot be a consistent Christian and be popular. It must be admitted that there are some situations where this literally would be true. However, it is not the case in many groups and communities and on many campuses. There are some places where uncompromisingly Christian young people can be and are among the most popular.

If we are not popular and not respected by most of our associates, should we not look within ourselves? If we will look closely enough, we may discover that our lack of popularity has resulted from faults within our own personalities. It may be that we are proud and egotistical. We may be too determined to have our own way. We may be obsessed with a reformer complex. Or, we may have a spirit of self-righteousness.

It may be correctly inferred from the preceding that it is legitimate for Christians to want to be liked and respected by others.

Some of you are very popular now; others of you are not. Whether popular or not, we can improve our personalities so they can be more effective channels for service.

CONCLUSION

With the danger of repetition, let us make a few closing suggestions, some negative, others positive.

From the negative viewpoint:

We should never compromise on basic moral principles.

We should not seek to win friends by being weak but by being strong. To compromise will weaken rather than strengthen our influence for good.

We should learn, however, to stand for what is right in such a way as not to offend needlessly.

We shall tend to irritate and lose the friendship of others if we are too dogmatic, too argumentative, or manifest a holier-than-thou, superior attitude.

From the more positive viewpoint:

We should watch our personal appearance, being careful that we keep ourselves attractive and neat.

We should do our best to be genuine and sincere at all times and under all sorts of conditions.

We should cultivate an interest in others and in what they are doing.

We should seek to be unselfish, devoted to the welfare of others.

We should remember that there is no substitute for a genuine love for people, for all kinds of people.

We should be cheerful and should develop and maintain healthy attitudes toward life.

We should talk about our religion more than we do, but if we want to have much influence with our associates, we must walk our religion more than we talk it. The walking will make the talking more effective.

The main question is not "Have I succeeded or failed to be popular?" but rather "Have I succeeded or failed to use what influence I have for Christ and for Christian ends?"

18

VICTORY OVER TEMPTATIONS

There was a tradition among certain Indians that the spirit of one who was scalped entered into the warrior who scalped him. This made the warrior stronger and more courageous. Each victory gave additional strength for the next battle.

There is a sense in which this is true in life. Do you ever sing in your church the old song:

> Yield not to temptation
> For yielding is sin:
> Each victory will help you
> Some other to win.

Each victory will not assure victory the next time, but it will help you some other to win. The law of habit works both ways. Good habits, as well as bad habits, are made stronger by each repetition. Likewise, temptations and bad habits are weakened each time one has the victory over them.

Possibly some of the things we have discussed in the chapters of Part II represent real temptations to you. There may be other things even more serious for you, because they go deeper into your life and personality. Before we leave this section dealing with problems, let us consider briefly the whole matter of temptations and how we can have the victory over them.

RECOGNIZE THEIR SOURCES

One step and possibly the first one in a conquest of temptation is to recognize the possible sources of our temptations.

There is a sense in which God tests Christians or permits them to be tested, but he never tempts anyone to do evil. "Let no one say when he is tempted, I am tempted by God, for God cannot be tempted with evil and he himself tempts no one" (James 1:13). God's pull on man is toward the good rather than the evil.

There are three main sources of temptations, all interrelated in a sense. A knowledge of these will help us to strive more intelligently and successfully for victory in times of temptation.

The first of these sources is the devil. It was he who approached Eve in the form of the serpent. He led David to sin against God by numbering the people (1 Chron. 21:1). Jesus was "led up by the Spirit into the wilderness to be tempted by the devil" (Matt. 4:1). Paul advised the Ephesians to put on the whole armor of God that they might be able "to stand against the wiles of the devil" (Eph. 6:11). Peter says, "Your adversary the devil prowls around like a roaring lion, seeking some one to devour" (1 Peter 5:8). In at least two places in the New Testament, Satan is called "the tempter" (Matt. 4:3; 1 Thess. 3:5).

Just as a Christian feels the sustaining strength of a power other than himself, so at times he feels that there is a power other than himself that is fighting against his best interests. Have you ever had that feeling? Paul evidently had such experiences. He wrote: "For we are not contending against flesh and blood, but against the principalities, against the powers, against the world rulers of this present darkness, against the spiritual hosts of wickedness in the heavenly places" (Eph. 6:12). The Christian must wage constant warfare against wicked, spiritual (non-physical) powers.

Most temptations have their immediate source in the spoken invitation, the attitude, or the example of some person. This is the second of the three sources of temptations. There are some people who wilfully seek to entice others into sin. The writer of Proverbs advises, "My son, if sinners entice you, do not consent" (Prov. 1:10). These enticers make it their business to make the temptation and the sin it would lead to as attractive as possible. They appeal to the young to come and have a "good time" but hide from them the ultimate consequences of sin.

Some of the most difficult temptations come through one's

friends or loved ones. It may not be a spoken appeal but the appeal of example. It may be the temptation to conform for the sake of uniformity and a good time. To yield means the surrender of ideals. Such a surrender may lead to a gradual lowering of all moral standards.

The third source of temptations is our own evil desires and weaknesses. Have you ever done anything wrong and immediately said to yourself, "That was not I; it must have been someone else?" All of us, at times, have the feeling that we are a Dr. Jekyll and a Mr. Hyde. There is something within us that responds to the appeal of the good; there is likewise something within us that responds to the appeal of the evil.

When one becomes a Christian the balance in his life is shifted toward the good, yet there continues to be something within him which can be appealed to by the evil. Jesus said to the tired, sleepy apostles, "Watch and pray that you may not enter into temptation; the spirit indeed is willing, but the flesh is weak" (Matt. 26:41). James says: "each person is tempted when he is lured and enticed by his own desire. Then desire when it has conceived gives birth to sin; and sin when it is full-grown brings forth death" (James 1:14–15).

We cannot shift the entire responsibility for our temptations and sins to others. We are led astray by our own evil desires. At times, we deliberately, premeditatedly enter into sin. Although temptation may come from outside ourselves, there is something within us that responds to it. The ultimate responsibility for our sins rests squarely upon us. We make our own decisions. Our wills are ours with which to say yes or no.

UNDERSTAND THEIR PURPOSES

The fact that God does not directly send temptations does not mean that he does not use them for his purposes. An understanding of the purposes for which God may use temptations will aid us, to a degree, in our effort to overcome them. We should not forget that they cannot serve God's purposes unless we have the victory over them.

Real happiness and abiding joy come to victors over temptation. "The most buoyant people we meet are those who refuse to be drowned by sorrow, or overcome by difficulty, or defeated by sin." The devil cannot have any happy old people; all the happy old people have had the joy of triumphal conquest over the baser desires of life.

Temptations if overcome will also develop character. The athlete develops his body by exercise and by overcoming physical resistance; the scholar trains his mind by tackling difficult intellectual problems and solving them; the Christian grows character by overcoming the temptations of life. There can be no moral triumph without moral struggle.

Christians should be the most courageous of people. The problems, the difficulties, and the temptations of life should not be permitted to defeat them. Their problems should be made stepping stones to higher levels of living, for the conquest of temptations is a part of the maturing process. Are we progressively having the victory over the temptations that would defeat us?

The type of football player we like is the one who plays his best when the opposition is the strongest. He grits his teeth, stiffens his back, and plays a little harder. We like the same kind of Christian.

The test of our lives is not whether or not we have had complete victory over the temptations of life, but what kind of a fight we are putting up to overcome the temptations that beset us. Is the direction of our lives away from sin rather than toward sin? This is the real test for our lives.

Temptations themselves serve as a means of testing us. A leading tire manufacturer has the slogan "Tested on the speedway for your safety on the highway." There are highly skilled pilots who put planes through the severest possible maneuvers before the plane is released for military or commercial service. In this way, imperfections and weaknesses may be revealed.

In much the same way, character is revealed by testing. There is no way of being sure of a life, whether it is ours or another's, until that life has been thoroughly tested. Just as a strong, sturdy oak cannot be grown in a hothouse, so strong Christian character cannot be developed in a spiritual vacuum. The Christian, if he is to grow, must meet squarely and have the victory over the tests and challenges of life.

Temptations to a Christian can and should serve another good purpose. They should make us conscious of our need of divine help. The experiences we have had with temptations prove to us that we fail when we attempt to meet in our own strength the challenges of the devil and our own corrupt nature. The glorious thing, however, is that when we turn to our Heavenly Father for the necessary assistance, we always find him adequate.

CONDITIONS FOR CONQUEST

If we expect to have progressively the victory over temptations, we must meet certain conditions.

If we want to have the victory, we must avoid temptations whenever we can wisely do so. There may arise occasions when it would be cowardly not to face some temptation squarely, but it is foolhardy to place ourselves needlessly in situations that tempt us to do wrong. That is one count against some of the problems we have discussed. To participate in them frequently involves one in many other temptations.

The Christian, particularly the young Christian, should heed the advice of the wise man: "Do not enter the path of the wicked, and do not walk in the way of evil men" (Prov. 4:14).

We should remember that Jesus taught his disciples to pray "And lead us not into temptation. But deliver us from evil."

Although we may seek, in every legitimate way, to avoid temptations; nevertheless, we shall face plenty of them. If we are to have the victory over them, we must believe that victory is possible.

Victories on the athletic field, in the field of military combat, or in life's battles are won by those who believe they can win. Most battles, before they are fought, are decided within the minds and hearts of the combatants. Christians can be and should be victorious over temptations. We are not supposed to live defeated lives.

In his contest with the devil, Jesus came out victor every time. Luke, in closing his account of the temptation of Jesus, said, "And when the devil had ended every temptation, he departed from him until an opportune time" (Luke 4:13). Jesus had many temptations which are not recorded. He "in every respect has been tempted as we are, yet without sinning" (Heb. 4:15). Notice what the writer adds: "Let us then with confidence draw near to the throne of grace, that we may receive mercy and find grace to help in time of need." Tempted "in every respect" is our assurance of a sympathetic Saviour; "yet without sinning" is our assurance of victory. We have the strength of the Master at our command.

Paul, writing to the Christians in one of the most wicked cities of that time, said, "No temptation has overtaken you that is not common to man. God is faithful, and he will not let you be tempted beyond your strength, but with the temptation will also provide the way of escape, that you may be able to endure it" (1 Cor. 10:13).

Another thing that will help us to have the victory is to remember Dad and Mother, our pastor and teacher, our friend or sweetheart, who have confidence in us and are depending upon us.

> I would be true, for there are those who trust me;
> I would be pure, for there are those who care;
> I would be strong, for there is much to suffer;
> I would be brave, for there is much to dare.

In addition to our loved ones and friends we can be sure that Jesus is depending upon us. How can we as Christians, when we remember what he has done for us, be untrue to such a friend as he?

> Jesus is all the world to me,
> And true to Him I'll be;
> Oh, how could I this Friend deny,
> When He's so true to me?

An additional condition for victory is for us to keep busy doing good. Paul says, "Do not be overcome by evil, but overcome evil with good" (Rom. 12:20). It may be that Paul is talking about our relation to evil outside of ourselves, but the admonition is just as true of the evil desires and purposes of our own inner selves.

Minds and hearts, hands and feet that are kept busy thinking good and doing good will not have time to do evil. This "good" should include both activity for the Lord and fellowship with him. If we are busy in Sunday school, in our church youth organizations, and in wholesome school and community activities, the occasions for serious temptations will be greatly reduced. This will be particularly true if we take some time each day for fellowship with our Heavenly Father through Bible study, prayer, and meditation.

Still another condition for victory, which has already been suggested, is that we must fight against temptations when they come. The Christian life is a hotly contested game, a constant warfare. Victory cannot be expected without a fight. The Christian is to "resist the devil" (James 4:7); to strive or struggle (an athletic term) against sin (Heb. 12:4); to put on the "whole armor of God" (Eph. 6:13).

Standards of right and wrong must be intelligently erected, ideals of personal conduct should be carefully set up. These standards and ideals should be defended at any cost. The fight may be hard, but the victory will be worth it. God's assurance of victory is given only to the courageous, fighting heart. We can be certain God will do his part; will we do ours? Are we going to be a weakling, drifting along with whatever crowd we happen to be in, or are we going to have the grit and the courage to buck the crowd when that crowd is wrong? Our answer to that question is important.

Let us re-emphasize that drifters are never lifters. They never start a current in the opposite direction. Drifters are lost in the current. Lifters stand out from the crowd and become the leaders of men for God and righteousness.

> We rise by the things that are under our feet,
> By what we have mastered of good or gain,
> By the pride deposed and the passion slain
> And the vanquished ills that we hourly meet.

We may meet all of the preceding conditions for conquest over temptation and yet fail because we do not let the Lord fight with us. His power alone is stronger than sin. "Where sin increased, grace abounded all the more" (Rom. 5:20). Paul prayed to the Lord three times to remove his thorn in the flesh, which more than likely was some physical handicap but which may have been a special temptation or besetting sin. The Lord's reply was, "My grace is sufficient for you, for my power is made perfect in weakness" (2 Cor. 12:9). Peter, often tempted and tried, spoke from experience when he said, "the Lord knows how to rescue the godly from trial" (2 Peter 2:9).

Victory will come to us when we want it enough to bow before the Lord and ask his help and have enough faith to believe that he can and will help. It is then that we can say with Paul, "I can do all things in him who strengthens me" (Phil. 4:13).

Part III

POSITIVE CHRISTIAN
LIVING

19

RELIGION: NEGATIVE AND POSITIVE

The problems discussed in Part II represent, in the main, what some choose to call the "negatives" of the Christian life. It was felt that this study of "right or wrong" would not be complete without some emphasis on the more positive expressions of the Christian religion. The chapters of Part III are dedicated to this purpose. It is hoped that they will represent the climax of our study together. It is believed that a prayerful study of these chapters will help you to discover some principles that will guide you in your decisions, even concerning the "negatives" of life.

In the present chapter, we shall consider the place and relative importance of the negative and the positive emphases. We do not want you to conclude, from reading Part II, that we consider the negative the most important aspect of the Christian's life.

This is definitely not true, although the negative is an essential part of any well-rounded, effective Christian life. But it is possible that, at a particular stage of the development of an individual Christian, some decision in the area of the negative may be immediately the most important decision he can make. We may discover in this matter, as in so many other areas of life, that it is not an "either . . . or" but a "both . . . and." When properly interpreted, we may see that both the negative and the positive have an important place in any adequate expression of the Christian way of life.

THE GOOD CHRISTIAN

Before we consider specifically the negative and positive aspects of the Christian life, it may be wise to attempt to answer the question "What makes one a good Christian?"

There have been, historically, and are, in the contemporary

period, several answers to this question. Some say that the good Christian is one who is sound or orthodox in his beliefs. In contrast, there are other people who say "It doesn't make any difference what you believe; it is what you do."

As is usually true, somewhere between these two extremes is the best or correct position. It does make considerable difference what one believes concerning some things. For example, what one believes in regard to God, Christ, the Bible, man, sin, salvation, and the church, makes a great deal of difference. There is wrapped up potentially enough in our beliefs concerning these and closely related subjects to determine what we become, what will be the motivating drives in our lives, and what will be our contribution to the world.

However, the ultimate goodness and worth of a Christian involves more than what he believes. It is possible for him to be orthodox, at least theoretically, in his beliefs, while at the same time he may be a very poor example of what a Christian should be.

A second answer frequently given to the question "What makes one a good Christian?" is faithfulness to the formal requirements of his religion. In other words, one who is faithful in his attendance at the services of his church and gives liberally of his time, talents, and money to support and to promote the program of his church and the cause of Christ, is judged to be a good Christian.

There is much validity to this claim. Such a person will usually be a good Christian. However, this is not necessarily true. There is even a possibility that faithfulness to the formal requirements of one's religion may be used as a substitute for a consistent Christian life.

We believe that we speak the mind of the Lord when we say that the substitute is not acceptable unto him. It was not in the days of the prophets and Jesus. The theme of prophetic religion was: "Has the Lord as great delight in burnt offerings and sacrifices, as in obeying the voice of the Lord? Behold, to obey is better than sacrifice, and to hearken than the fat of rams" (1 Sam.

15:22; cf. Isa. 1:10–17 and Amos 5:21–24). Formal religion was not sufficient. God wanted then and wants now something that goes deeper, that is more meaningful. The sacrifice, the worship, the service is acceptable to God only if it is in harmony with one's inner attitudes toward God and his outer relations with his fellow man.

A third general answer that is frequently given to the question, "What makes one a good Christian?" is that it is the kind or quality of life he lives. Most of us will agree that this is the best test of whether or not one is a real Christian. Jesus himself said, "You will know them by their fruits" (Matt. 7:16), while James said, "Show me your faith apart from your works, and I by my works will show you my faith" (James 2:18).

We should remember, however, that the best Christian will be sound in the faith. He will conscientiously observe the formal requirements of his religion. Then he will add to these a consistent life for Christ. This everyday Christian living represents "the weightier matters of the law, justice and mercy and faith [or integrity—Goodspeed]" (Matt. 23:23).

Living the Christian life, if it is to be most effective, must be a twenty-four hours a day, seven days a week job. There is no thirty-, forty-, or even sixty-hour week for the real Christian.

There are two emphases that properly may be made concerning consistent Christian living. These are the negative and positive emphases. Some people tend to judge the Christian's life largely in terms of what he does not do, while others give primary emphasis to what he does or to the quality of life revealed in his day-by-day contacts with others.

Some, who give the positive emphasis first place, judge a man's religion largely in terms of his relation to other individuals, while others emphasize primarily his attitude toward and his work on behalf of certain social and moral issues of the day.

THE PLACE OF THE NEGATIVE

What place does and should the negative emphasis have in the Christian life? We know, of course, that the "thou shalt nots" are very prominent in the Old Testament. All but two of the Ten Commandments are stated negatively.

Some Christians argue, however, that we are no longer under the law, that we are under grace. They suggest that the negative emphasis belonged to the childhood period of the race. To substantiate their general position, they cite the life and teachings of Jesus who had little place in his ministry for the "thou shalt nots."

There is one thing that such people may fail to remember about Jesus: He did not deal with many specific problems. He was satisfied, in the main, to set out general principles that have been abidingly valid. One reason for their continuous validity is the fact that, with rare exceptions, he did not apply them specifically to particular situations. When one applies even positive principles to specific situations, he frequently gives a negative emphasis to them.

The negative had a much more prominent place in the writings and the ministry of Paul than in the life and teachings of Jesus. Paul was dealing with particular situations. He was faced with very real problems of real people in the churches he had founded and to whom he ministered and wrote. Most of these people lacked the background of training in the Old Testament law that was common to most Jews. If one who does not believe in teaching and preaching "the negatives" of the Christian life reads Paul's epistles carefully, he would find that he stood corrected.

The suggestion has been made that some claim that the negative emphasis belongs to the childhood period. This is correct. One sign of maturity—biological, emotional, and spiritual—is the fact that one accentuates or emphasizes the positive phases of life more and the negative less. But who would dare say that we are so mature that we no longer need some emphasis on the negatives of the Christian life?

We shall not be prepared, however, to proceed to the more positive, mature type of Christian life, unless we have had a real victory in the area of the negatives. The victories in that area are essential to the maturing process. This is the reason we implied earlier that it is possible that a decision not to do a certain thing may be, at that particular time, the most important decision of our lives. It may set the direction of our lives. It may be the fore-runner of other and more important decisions. At least we must be willing to follow the Lord in regard to the negatives of life, before we can expect him to find full expression in us and through us in the positive phases of our lives.

I believe you will agree that there are many members of our churches who are mature in years but very immature as Chris-tians. Many of them need the negative emphases as much as, if not more than, those of you who are much younger. There are few things, if any, that are hurting the spiritual life of our churches and reducing their impact on the world any more than the com-promising lives of so many church members—young and old.

THE PLACE OF THE POSITIVE

We have emphasized a great deal, in the preceding chapters, the importance of the negative aspects of the Christian life. We should not forget, however, that it is possible, although not probable, that one may not smoke, drink, gamble, cheat, pet, dance, and so forth, and yet he may fail to be a good Christian. He may be merely good for nothing.

Paul not only instructed his converts to put off some things but also to put on some things (see Col. 3:1–14). The final test of how mature we are as Christians is how much the Spirit of Christ lives in us and finds expression through us in our relations with others. Do we have the qualities Paul says should characterize the one who has been raised with Christ? They are: "compassion, kind-ness, lowliness, meekness, and patience, forbearing one another and, if one has a complaint against another, forgiving each other; as the Lord has forgiven you, so you also must forgive." He then adds: "And above all these put on love, which binds everything together in perfect harmony" (Col. 3:12–14). Do we manifest the fruit of the Spirit which is "love, joy, peace, patience, kindness, goodness, faithfulness, gentleness, self-control" (Gal. 5:22–23)?

Let us emphasize again that the positive is the supreme test of the mature Christian life, although it is never to be substituted for the negative aspects of that life. The negatives, as we mature, will disturb and concern us less and less. This will be true primarily because we have settled these matters and have gone on to more important things. I dare say that the Christians in your church, who count for most in the church and in the community, are those who no longer have to debate with themselves as to whether or not it is right or wrong for them to do most of the things that have been discussed in Part II. They have made decisions that are final for them concerning those things.

The preceding correctly implies a possible relationship between the settling of the negatives and the development of stable, positive, Christian character. Every decision we make concerning any negative angle of the Christian life will contribute, in one way or another, to the positive side of our Christian lives. On the other hand, as we develop along positive lines, we have a broader and sounder basis for our decisions concerning these negative matters.

There is at least one other thing that we should remember about the maturing process of the Christian life. One test of how mature we are is how much of the expression of the positive Christian life flows naturally and inevitably from an inner spirit that possesses us and how much of it results from outer pressure or personal discipline.

We have not arrived at spiritual maturity until the Spirit of Christ so lives in us that he expresses himself through us. As we mature, we become increasingly unconscious that our lives are influencing others for Christ. The best Christians in any church and community are largely unconscious that they are good. Christ so lives in them that others cannot help but see him incarnated in their lives. He has become a well of living water within them, flowing through them to bless all they touch. If we have constantly to make an effort to be good, the attempt itself is a sign of immaturity.

The preceding does not mean that we should cease all striving after goodness. No, so long as we are immature—and none of us ever reaches full maturity—we should make a conscious effort to live the Christian life. This we can do without any apology or embarrassment, knowing that it is the common lot of all Christians. Even Paul said: "Not that I have already obtained this or am already perfect; but I press on to make it my own, because Christ Jesus has made me his own. Brethren, I do not consider that I have made it my own; but one thing I do, forgetting what lies behind and straining forward to what lies ahead, I press on toward the goal for the prize of the upward call of God in Christ Jesus. Let those of us who are mature be thus minded; and if in anything you are otherwise minded, God will reveal that also to you. Only let us hold true to what we have attained" (Phil. 3:12–16).

What does all of this mean to you and me? It simply means that we shall continue unto the end of our earthly journey to be immature spiritually, in some way and to some degree. Full maturity would mean perfection.

This, in turn, means that we shall need to give some attention indefinitely to the "thou shalt nots" of the Christian life. We shall have to keep on making decisions concerning things we should or should not do. It also means that we shall need to continue to put forth conscious effort to be a good Christian, to give Christ a chance to express himself more fully through us.

It means, however, that we can measure our progress toward maturity by the direction in which our lives are moving. Are the negatives of decreasing and the positive phases of the Christian life of increasing significance and importance to us? Is less and less conscious effort required for us to live a decent Christian life?

20

A PERSONAL COVENANT

As we come to the close of this study, some of you may wish to make a tangible covenant with the Lord concerning some of the problems discussed and other matters of real concern to you. Or, it may be that you would like to renew a covenant you have made with the Lord in the past.

The outline in this chapter is provided for your convenience. Some of you may prefer to formulate your own statements. Do it any way you want to, but it is hoped that you will make some kind of a committal concerning those things most pertinent to your life.

If you use the check list, you may want to check the various statements in your book, or you may prefer to copy the list, check it, and place it in your Bible. Be sure to notice that you cannot check every item. In a few cases there are statements that are mutually exclusive.

Please approach this phase of our study together thoughtfully and prayerfully. For any decision to be most meaningful, it must be strictly personal and thoroughly sincere. Notice carefully the wording of the covenant preceding the check list.

MY COVENANT

Recognizing that I belong to the Lord and out of gratitude to him for all that he has done for me, I covenant, with his help, to strive to make the following promises, that I have voluntarily entered into, a vital part of my daily living for him. I promise—

1. Cheating
   ☐ That I will not cheat on tests and examinations.
   ☐ That I will not do unfair work on school assignments.

    ☐ That I will not aid others in cheating or unfair work.
2. Gambling
    ☐ That I will not gamble on athletic games.
    ☐ That I will avoid all other forms of gambling.
3. Movies
    ☐ That I will attend only carefully selected movies.
    ☐ That I will not attend the movies at all.
    ☐ That I will not attend the movies on Sunday.
4. Sunday observance
    ☐ That I will make no more purchases than absolutely necessary on Sunday.
    ☐ That I will participate only in activities on Sunday that are appropriate to the Lord's day.
5. Smoking
    ☐ That I will not use tobacco in any form.
    ☐ That I will tactfully encourage other young people to take the same position.
6. Drinking
    ☐ That I will never drink beverage alcohol in any form.
    ☐ That I will refuse to date those who drink.
    ☐ That I will participate, when possible, in educational and legislative programs to reduce the evils of beverage alcohol.
7. Dancing
    ☐ That although I now dance, I will seek honestly to know God's will for me concerning dancing.
    ☐ That I will not dance.
    ☐ That I will use my influence, in groups to which I belong, to have other activities substituted for dancing.
8. Petting
    ☐ That I will refuse to permit or to participate in petting.
    ☐ That I will seek to maintain the highest Christian standards on the dates I have.
9. Popularity
    ☐ That I will never compromise my Christian principles to increase my popularity.

☐ That I will use what popularity I have for Christ-honoring purposes.

10. Temptations and bad habits
   ☐ That I will ask God to give me strength to break one or more specific bad habits known to him and to me.
   ☐ That I will avoid the reading of literature that tempts me to think or to do wrong.

11. My personal devotional life
   ☐ That I will spend some time each day in Bible reading, prayer, and meditation.
   ☐ That I will have a prayer list of people and objects for which I will pray regularly.
   ☐ That I will seek to know the will of God in every time of decision.
   ☐ That I will open more fully every area of my life to the indwelling Christ.

12. My church life
   ☐ That I will be faithful in my attendance at the teaching, training, and worship services of my church.
   ☐ That I will invite others to my church: its services and its organizations.
   ☐ That I will be faithful to any church responsibility that I may have, whether it is small or great.
   ☐ That I will give at least a tithe of all that I make to support the cause of Christ.
   ☐ That I will recognize that all that I make and have belongs to God, and is to be used in ways approved by him.

13. Christian conduct
   ☐ That I will seek so to live before others that they will respect my religion.
   ☐ That I will be more considerate of others.
   ☐ That I will seek opportune times when I can speak to unsaved friends concerning the acceptance of Christ as Saviour and Lord.
   ☐ That I will keep my body in good condition, knowing that it is the temple of the Holy Spirit and that it is to be

presented to God as a living sacrifice, holy, acceptable unto him.

☐ That I will apply myself to my school work, recognizing it as an opportunity not only to prepare myself for the future but as a channel for Christian witnessing now.

☐ That I will be faithful to every work responsibility in the home and outside the home.

☐ That I will discipline myself, in such a way and to such a degree, that my desires and appetites will be controlled and expressed only in ways approved by God and by my own better self.

☐ That I will express the Christian spirit in my relations with the members of my family.

☐ That I will apply the Christian spirit and principles to current moral and social problems such as race relations.

☐ That I will seek the guidance of the Lord in choosing my vocation.

☐ That I will dedicate my vocation to the good of man and the glory of God.

☐ That I will ask God's leadership in the choice of my life's companion.

☐ That I will do what I can to promote the cause of Christ among men, to the ends of the earth and in every area of life.

14. Others of your own choosing

Part IV

A POSTSCRIPT

21

CHALLENGED BY CHRIST

No person, young or old, ever reaches the full potential of his personality until he ties his life on to some cause or program bigger than himself; a cause or a program to which he can and will unselfishly give his life.

Christianity, if it is to solve the problems of the contemporary period and to meet the challenge of communism, must recapture the spirit of martyrdom, which characterized it in its early days and in the most glorious periods of its history. It must inspire its adherents to a sacrificial devotion comparable to the fanatical zeal of the followers of Marx, Lenin, and Stalin. The fact that organized Christianity has failed, to such a large degree, to present the challenge that is in Christ is one of the major factors in the rise of such modern "isms" as fascism and communism.

The Christian movement, in its times of inner renewal, has gone back to its original sources. It has returned to Jesus and to his simple but challenging principles and ideals. It has sought to recover the sense of his presence and the urgency of his call. Such a return to Jesus is needed desperately in our day. Let us as individuals return unto him that we may be challenged to live courageously and creatively for him in our world.

CHALLENGED BY HIS INVITATION

When two of the disciples of John the Baptist asked Jesus "Rabbi (which means Teacher), where are you staying?," his answer was "Come and see" (John 1:38–39). This is the continuing invitation of Jesus. If we doubt him in any way, let us come unto him and see if he will not challenge us, inspire us, and lift us out of our selfish purposes and ambitions. Let us see if he will not give us new insights into his will, enlarged dreams of what we should do for him and our fellow man, and the drive and power to make our dreams a reality.

The two disciples of John the Baptist who went home with Jesus that day were Andrew and John. They found and brought to Jesus their brothers, Simon and James. This happened in Judea.

A short time later Jesus was going by the shores of the Sea of Galilee and saw Simon and Andrew casting a net into the sea. He said to them, "Follow me, and I will make you fishers of men" (Matt. 4:19). He gave a similar invitation to John and James, who were in a boat with Zebedee their father. Notice that the invitation of Jesus was "Follow me." Jesus not only invites men and women to come unto him but also to follow him.

There must have been something about his bearing, his look, his voice, and doubtless his previous contacts with these fishermen brothers, that caused them to leave immediately their nets and follow him. Jesus is going somewhere and everywhere in the world; we cannot come unto him and stay in his presence unless we follow him, unless we go with him where he is going.

Notice also that he said, "Follow me, and I will make you fishers of men." Jesus is in the business of making or remaking people. Under the impact of the life and spirit of Jesus, Simon, the hot-headed fisherman, became Peter, the rock, the one who preached the matchless message of salvation to thousands on the day of Pentecost. James, the son of Thunder, became the first martyr among the disciples, and John his brother became the one who leaned on the breast of Jesus at the Last Supper. He will make or remake us if we will let him.

Jesus promised to make them fishers of men. He promised to bless and to use the skills they had perfected as fishermen to catch and win men for him. Whatever our abilities, our skills, our training, he can and will take what we have and use it in his service if we will follow him.

Let us never forget that the initial invitation of Jesus is, "Come, follow me." There is a tremendous challenge in it. If we do not think so, let us sincerely and searchingly ask ourselves, "What would it mean in my life if I really followed Jesus?"

Let us not forget that he will never force us to follow him. He will and does lay down the conditions that we must meet if we are to follow him. It is up to us to accept or to reject his invitation. What is our answer?

The purpose of his invitation is revealed in the simple statement concerning the appointment of the twelve. It says, "And he appointed twelve, to be with him, and to be sent out . . ." (Mark 3:14). They were to be with him that they might have fellowship with him and he with them. But this fellowship was primarily preparatory. The ultimate purpose was that they might be sent out to preach or witness for him. So it is in our lives. The invitation is to come unto him, but the invitation carries in it a challenging command to go.

CHALLENGED BY HIS IDEALS

We do not have the space to discuss all the ideals or principles of Jesus. In this section we shall restrict our consideration to his ideal of perfection. There is a sense in which every fundamental principle of Jesus is an ideal of perfection. We shall give attention here, however, only to his specific teachings concerning individual and social perfection. When properly understood this ideal or those ideals will challenge us to the end of life's journey. They provide an abiding basis for judging our lives as his followers.

The ideal for the individual is found in the last verse of Matthew 5. Jesus had spoken the Beatitudes unto the people and had compared his disciples to salt and light. Following a rather extensive comparison of his principles with the Old Testament law and the Jewish interpretations of that law, the chapter reaches the climax in verse 48. Williams translates the verse as follows: "So you, my followers, ought to be perfect, as your heavenly Father is." Thus, Christ's ideal for the individual was and is perfection.

Perfection is also his ideal for society. It is most specifically stated in the prayer he taught his disciples. The first petition in the prayer is: Thy kingdom come, thy will be done, on earth as it is in heaven (Matt. 6:10).

Certainly, if his will were done on earth as it is in heaven, it would mean perfection. This is the ideal for which we are to pray and work. His kingdom, which for practical purposes can be equated with his reign or will, is, for his followers, to be the treasure hid in a field, the pearl of great value (Matt. 13:44–46). Its attainment is to be life's supreme goal. Seeking first his kingdom and his righteousness, we are to trust him to provide for us the necessities of life (Matt. 6:33).

We can argue long and loud about the possibility or the impossibility of attaining perfection for ourselves and for our society, but a more important question is whether or not we are making progress toward perfection. The supreme test of our lives is not our attainment but the direction of our lives. Are we headed in the right direction? Are we moving toward the ideal? Are we closer to it today than yesterday, this month than last month, this year than last year?

There is a deep and abiding challenge in the ideals of Jesus, ideals that never can be completely achieved in this life. An ideal that could be reached in a year, ten years, or a lifetime would not be continually challenging. In this sense, the impossible ideal is the most practical ideal.

CHALLENGED BY HIS EXAMPLE

The world has had many great moral and religious teachers, but the greatest by far was and is Jesus of Nazareth. His teachings are superior in many ways, but the most unique element in his teachings was the fact that he exemplified perfectly in his own life everything he taught.

This was even true of his ideal of perfection. He was tempted in all points like we are yet was without sin. Perfection, however, includes more than freedom from overt sin. It means complete harmony with the will and purpose of God. Jesus fulfilled this requirement. He came not to do his own will but the will of the

One who had sent him. He could truthfully say, without any pretense, "He that hath seen me hath seen the Father." This was true because he was the only Son of the Father. It was also true because, as the human Jesus, his will had become so completely identified with the Father's will that the two were one.

Men can and will find some fault with our lives and the lives of the best of God's saints, but when they examine the life of Jesus, they are forced to the conclusion of Pilate, "I find no fault in this man" (Luke 23:4 ASV).

What a challenge to attempt, as best we can, to follow him! It was Jesus himself who said, "As the Father has sent me, even so I send you" (John 20:21). In his prayer for his disciples he prayed, "As thou didst send me into the world, so I have sent them into the world . . . so that the world may believe that thou hast sent me" (John 17:18, 21).

Jesus was sent into the world to reveal the Father and to redeem man. In like manner, we are sent into the world to reveal Jesus to the world and to be a redeeming influence in the world. As he was God incarnate, so we are to be the incarnation of Christ that others, looking at the revelation of him in us, may believe that the Father sent him.

CHALLENGED BY HIS COMMISSION

In the beginning of his earthly ministry the invitation of Jesus was "Come unto me." At the end of his earthly journey his command was "Go . . . and make disciples of all nations." It is true that he told his disciples to tarry or stay in Jerusalem "until you are clothed with power from on high" (Luke 24:49). The staying or tarrying was absolutely essential, but it was preparatory. After the power came through the enduement of the Holy Spirit, they were to be his witnesses in Jerusalem, Judea, Samaria, and to the end of the earth (Acts 1:8).

What a daring commission! You are familiar with Matthew's record of it. Jesus gave to the little group, possibly just the eleven apostles and at the most not more than five hundred, a program of world conquest. They were to make disciples or learners of all nations. Those who were enlisted as disciples were to be baptized and, thus, to become identified with Christ's movement. Those won and baptized were to be taught to observe all that he had commanded them. To those who would thus go in obedience to his command he promised his abiding presence (Matt. 28:19–20).

Here are our marching orders. This is our task. Talk about a program that is challenging; neither communism nor any other "ism" has anything comparable to it. Our task is not complete until we have reached and won to Christ the last lost man in the darkest corner of the earth and until we have led him and all others won to apply Christ's spirit and his teachings to every area of their lives.

When the challenge that is in Christ and his program for us and our world grips our lives, does it not make many of our questions concerning right and wrong pale into insignificance? If we would respond courageously to his challenge, most of our questions would be answered for us.

It is the supreme task of each one of us to discover for ourselves what our particular place is to be in Christ's program of world conquest and world reconstruction. We should dedicate our talents, our time, our material possessions, ourselves to the promotion of the kingdom of God among men. This should be just as true of the housewife, the teacher, the banker, the farmer as it is of the preacher and the missionary. The supreme question of our lives should be, "Lord, what wilt thou have me to do?" Once we hear his voice, like Isaiah, we should cry out, "Here am I! Send me" (Isa. 6:8). At the end of our life's journey may we be able to say, as Paul did, "I was not disobedient to the heavenly vision."

> Lead on, O King Eternal!
> Till sin's fierce war shall cease,
> And holiness shall whisper
> The sweet Amen of peace;
> For not with swords loud clashing,
> Nor roll of stirring drums;
> But deeds of love and mercy
> The heav'nly kingdom comes.
>   Ernest W. Shurtleff